Turning Point

Turning Point

Joyce D. Weinsheimer

University of Minnesota

Wadsworth Publishing Company
Belmont, California
A Division of Wadsworth, Inc.

Printed in the United States of America

10 9 8 7 6 5 4 3 2 1

Library of Congress Cataloging-in-Publication Data
Weinsheimer, Joyce D., [date]
    Turning point / Joyce D. Weinsheimer.
      p. cm.
    Includes bibliographical references and index.
    ISBN 0-534-19422-2
    1. College attendance—United States.   1. Study, Method of.
3. College students—United States—Attitudes.   I. Title.
LC148.2.W45   1992
378.1'702812—dc20   92-14331
                                                               CIP

Sponsoring Editor: *Claire Verduin*
Marketing Representative: *Dean Allsman*
Editorial Associate: *Gay C. Bond*
Production Editor: *Marjorie Z. Sanders*
Manuscript Editor: *Kirk Bomont*
Permissions Editor: *Karen Wootten*
Interior Design and Typesetting: *Scratchgravel Publishing Services*
Cover Design: *Samuel Miranda*
Printing and Binding: *Malloy Lithographing, Inc.*

To my parents, Art and Hester Eaton,
to my husband, Joel,
to my children, Aaron and Amy

A portion of the proceeds from this book will be donated to the Resource Lab of the Learning & Academic Skills Center at the University of Minnesota.

Preface

Every term colleges place thousands of students on scholastic probation. By notifying these students of their probationary status, the college delivers the message that its standards are not being met and that students should get involved with the resources available to support their academic success. How do students react to this news?

Some students quickly dismiss their probationary status with the remark "This really isn't a problem. I'll go back next term and things will be different." Some students are shocked by the news. "How could this happen to me? I'm an intelligent person!" Others respond by blaming the system: "How can anyone do well at this college? It's just too difficult to learn here!" Still others feel embarrassed, wondering what people will think of them. A few even believe that nothing they do will make any difference and that their suspension is inevitable.

Though it's understandable that students may start with these reactions to their probationary status, it is in the interest of neither the institution nor the students when they get stuck with them. If students think that the problem of academic difficulty will go away on its own or that it can't be solved, they won't try anything new. If they feel ashamed or fear that exposing their probationary status to others could make them appear inadequate, they may not look for help. If they believe that it is impossible to succeed in a particular class or learn from a certain teacher, then they may not be willing to experiment with different strategies for learning.

Since we want students to get off academic probation and on with their education, we need to do more than simply inform them that all is not well. *Turning Point* is a tool that gives students a chance to put failure in perspective and take charge of the future. This book helps students (1) determine what obstacles are interfering with their learning, (2) devise a plan to overcome them, and (3) gain the self-confidence and self-determination they need to succeed in college. Whether used as a classroom text, in discussions with an adviser, or as part of a self-help program, this book sets the stage for academic improvement.

Because the reasons for academic difficulty in higher education are complex, the solution for getting off probation may vary from one individual to another. Most important about this book is that students are encouraged to go beyond generalities as they search for a way to turn their own situations around. Rather than frustrate students with a generic prescription for success that may not produce results for them, *Turning Point* helps students figure out what makes learning in college difficult in their case. The book's directed exercises in self-reflection, titled "Looking in the Mirror," enable students to produce pertinent answers that work.

Acknowledgments

Many people deserve thanks for their help with this book.

I am grateful to Elizabeth Wales, Director of University Counseling Services, and Nick Barbatsis, Associate Vice President of Student Affairs at the University of Minnesota, for supporting my research in learning assistance and for the gift of time to devote to this effort.

A special word of thanks is due to Barbara Becker, Director of Student Academic Support Services, and William Beyer, Coordinator of Premajor Advising, for making possible my work with College of Liberal Arts students on academic probation.

Appreciation for their helpful reviews and suggestions goes to Thomas Upton and Glenn Hirsch, my colleagues in the Learning & Academic Skills Center; to Susan Gekas, Normandale Community College; Karen G. Smith, Rutgers, the State University of New Jersey; Melinda Steele, Texas Tech University; and to students on probation at the University of Minnesota.

I thank Lisa Hirdler for her assistance with the manuscript and for her willingness to add yet another typing project to her very full schedule.

Finally, I am indebted to my husband, Joel, whose encouragement made the completion of this book possible.

Joyce D. Weinsheimer

Contents

Introduction

This book is written for college students who are on probation and want to get off.

Students who are glad that they're on probation and look forward to leaving at the end of the term should read no further. If you're simply putting in your time until the college says "Out!" this book is not for you.

If, on the other hand, you think you'd like to earn your degree and are wondering how to make that happen, read on. You'll find ideas to consider, questions to ask, and strategies to try. Since there's no single formula for doing well in college, this book will not tell you "the way" to graduate. Instead, it will help you figure out an approach to college that works for you.

Turning Point is a worktext, which means that you get to do some of the thinking and writing. Completing the exercises gives you a chance to personalize the information you read. And because your circumstances and experiences are unique to you, you need to take an active part in figuring out what you will do next. After all, nobody can do it for you, and nobody can tell in advance what will work best for you. So use this book as a practical tool to explore your options for getting what you want, and start getting off probation and on with your education today.

PART ONE

Dealing with Academic Probation

1

Getting the News

How are you reacting to the news that you're on academic probation?

Some students quickly dismiss their probationary status with a shrug, remarking "This really isn't a problem. I'll go back next term and things will be different." Some students are shocked by the news: "How could this happen to me? I'm an intelligent person!" Others blame the system: "How can anyone do well at this place? The courses are boring and the instructors are terrible!" Still others feel embarrassed, wondering what people will think of them. A few even believe that nothing they do will make any difference and that their suspension is inevitable.

Let's take a look at some reactions of students who are just finding out that they're on probation.

Bob opens the letter from his college, knowing that the news will not be good. Hard courses in both English and math made this term a rough one. Friends visiting his new apartment constantly interrupted his study time, and working a part-time job to cover expenses took time away from classes as well. "Too much to do in too little time," thinks Bob. "But no big deal. I just need to get my act together."

Maria scans the terms of her probation in amazement. How could she have moved so quickly from being at the top of her high school class to getting a letter like this? Grade reports that only a year ago had measured her progress with grades of "A" and "B" now regularly contain grades of "C" and "D." "And here's an 'F' in Physics," groans a frustrated Maria. "I'm too smart to be getting these grades. I should be doing a lot better."

Sara throws her academic status letter on the floor and stomps over to a chair. How dare that history instructor give her an 'F' for the term? She certainly wasn't going to make an appointment to talk with an advisor about her academic problem when the real problem was a teacher whose droning on about the Middle Ages put entire classes to sleep. And what about that foreign teaching assistant in calculus who couldn't even speak English? Who could learn anything in a class like that?

Looking over his announcement of probationary status, John feels sick. What will his parents think? His friends? All those people who just a few months ago wished him well in college? How can he go home and tell them that he is failing? In fact, how can he even face his new friends in college? "Everybody else seems to be doing fine," he concludes. "Talking about my low grades will just spread the word about the mess I'm in here. I had better figure out a way to handle this on my own."

Jan sets her probation letter on the table, thinking about the time she has left at the college. Should she finish the year? She certainly isn't getting the grades she wants, though she does enjoy attending classes and meeting new people. "But why take more courses if I'm eventually going to be suspended?" she wonders. "Maybe attending classes is a luxury I can't afford."

If you want to graduate from college, you must realize that though you may start with one of these reactions, you don't want to get stuck in it. Denying the seriousness of the situation may just pave the way from probation to suspension. On the other hand, going into shock or despair is not helpful either. And just recycling your reaction over and over again in your head doesn't get you anywhere.

Instead, consider your news about probation as a red flag: something is not going well. Face the news and consider your options. Then put your energy into getting what you want and going where you want to go.

Mario reads over the information about his probationary status, feeling disappointed. He had suspected that the term was not going to end on a positive note, though he had hoped that the grades on his final exams would help him out. "This news is not what I need," thinks Mario. "Guess it's time to find out what's going wrong and make some changes. I do want to get my degree, and right now I'm getting nowhere fast."

At the end of each chapter, "*Looking in the Mirror*" gives you a chance to reflect on some of the ideas you've just read about. Take the time to sort through your thoughts and answer the questions. Doing so will help you find your own personal path to college success.

Think back to when you first found out that you were on probation. What was your first reaction to the news? What thoughts went through your mind? Jot down a few sentences about how you felt.

When I first learned that I was on probation, I_____

_____

_____

_____

_____

_____

_____

2

Catching the Signal

When your car is about to fall apart, it usually gets your attention by lighting up one of the gauges on the instrument panel or by making weird noises. If you don't have a great love of repair shops or if your budget is tight, you may give the car a little extra time to let you know whether the problem is "significant" or not. But when the warnings persist, you finally "catch the signal"—you realize that something definitely is wrong and you consult a mechanic for diagnosis and treatment.

We've learned that we should pay attention to such signals and that we should consult an expert when we're not sure that all is well. But it may not be quite as clear how to handle signals indicating academic difficulty.

For example, when students consistently earn low grades or do not complete coursework, the signal indicating that all is not well often arrives in the form of a probation letter. The letter outlines the conditions that students must meet in order to remain at the college. It may also inform students about campus resources available for assistance. Yet how do students respond to this signal?

The students we met in Chapter 1 began by interpreting the news. That is, they went beyond the information about grades and requirements contained in the letter and made some assumptions about the causes and effects of their academic difficulties. Because thoughts about probation can be either helpful or harmful, it's important to be aware of your particular assumptions and their potential influence on the choices you make.

Let's take a closer look at some typical assumptions, which are listed below. How might each viewpoint affect how a student reacts to the probation signal? Briefly explain how each assumption might help or hinder someone who's wondering what to do about being on probation.

1. **College students should handle problems on their own.** Once you have graduated from high school, you are an adult. It is your responsibility to take care of problems that arise.

   Thinking this way might be useful to a student if _____

   _____

   _____

   _____

   _____

   _____

   One of the pitfalls of thinking this way might be that _____

   _____

   _____

   _____

   _____

   _____

2. **Academic probation means failure.** You are not currently meeting the academic standards of your institution. By not doing well in

your coursework, you are losing your opportunity to continue in higher education.

Thinking this way might be useful to a student if _____

_____

_____

_____

_____

One of the pitfalls of thinking this way might be that _____

_____

_____

_____

_____

3. **Intelligent students always succeed.** If you are smart enough to get into college, you can graduate.

Thinking this way might be useful to a student if _____

_____

_____

_____

_____

One of the pitfalls of thinking this way might be that _____

_____

_____

_____

_____

_____

4. **Failure is inevitable when learning conditions are less than ideal.** How much you learn and how well you do in higher education depends on the quality of the instruction and availability of academic support at your college.

Thinking this way might be useful to a student if _____

_____

_____

_____

_____

_____

One of the pitfalls of thinking this way might be that _____

_____

_____

_____

_____

5. **Students who fail let everyone down.** Enrolling in higher education is like making a public statement that you intend to earn a college degree. You agree to participate in the educational experiences your college offers and to meet its academic standards. When you fail, you let down the college that admitted you, the people that give you emotional and financial support, and yourself.

Thinking this way might be useful to a student if _____

_____

_____

_____

_____

One of the pitfalls of thinking this way might be that _____

_____

_____

_____

_____

As you can see from these assumptions, what students think about probation has an impact on how they feel about themselves and on what they do. If students feel ashamed or fear that exposing their probationary status to others will make them appear inadequate, they may not look for help. If they believe that it is impossible to succeed in a particular class or learn from a certain teacher, they may not be willing to experiment with different strategies for learning. If they think that the problem of academic difficulty will go away on its own or that it can't be solved, they won't try anything new.

Catching the signal requires setting aside interpretations that cloud your perception of the news about probation. It's not that these interpretations are bad or necessarily represent faulty thinking. But if your interpretations prevent you from clearly seeing what you need to do to accomplish your goals, then they are not useful to you. And if they direct your energy away from doing the things that could change your situation, then they are not useful to you either. If you want to graduate, let go of those thoughts and feelings that keep you from achieving this goal. Catch the signal, and get on with it!

One of the reasons it's difficult to respond to the probation signal is that people's thoughts about failure tend to be pretty muddled. Have you been told that "smart people don't make mistakes"? Have you also been told that "smart people learn from their mistakes"? Look at these mixed messages in light of your own experience with learning and you will realize why it's so difficult to think clearly about probation. Taking the time to unravel your own thoughts about probation gives you a chance to choose an effective response.

When I think about my probationary status, I assume it means that

_____

_____

_____

_____

_____

_____

_____

_____

_____

The usefulness of this thinking to me is that it _____

_____

_____

_____

_____

_____

Pitfalls of thinking this way might be that _____

_____

_____

_____

_____

Catching the signal means taking control and choosing my reaction to probation. The reaction that would give me the most power would be

_____

_____

_____

_____

_____

This reaction would help me get what I want because _____

_____

_____

_____

_____

_____

_____

_____

_____

_____

3

Understanding the Message

Now that you've started to sort through how you as an individual react to probation, let's consider once more the "news" you received from your college. Do you know the conditions of your probationary status? What do you need to do in order to work your way off probation? Do you need to complete a certain number of courses by a particular time? What grades do you need to earn? Are you expected to consult with any college personnel about being on probation?

Though the style may vary, all probation letters alert students to the fact that they are not meeting the academic standards of the college. The language may be formal, and the criteria listed for continuing at the college may be confusing. But when you cut through the institutional jargon, chances are the letter says something like this:

Dear _____:

Hey! What's going on? Your progress in this college is not what we expected! Remember that if you want to stick around here as a full-time student, you need to complete a certain number of credit hours each term and earn satisfactory grades.

If you don't meet these conditions, we can't let you continue to enroll in courses. It's unethical for us to keep taking your money when you're not making progress toward a degree.

Since none of us has been trained in fortune telling, we can't tell why you're having academic difficulty just from looking at your transcript. Maybe if you make an appointment to come in and talk over your situation with us, we can figure something out together. All we know right now is that something has got to change. We'll leave it up to you to decide what the next step is though, because it's your life.

Count on us for support if you want it. DO BETTER NEXT TERM.

Sincerely,

Your College Staff

If your letter sounded a little different from this one, remember that letters about probation are designed to impress you with the seriousness of your situation so that you will do something about it. It's understandable that the tone of such letters tends to be grim and bureaucratic—after all, the possibility of your leaving represents a no-win situation. The college believes that both you *and* they lose if you don't make it all the way to graduation. That's why they encourage you to meet with college staff to discuss your progress toward a degree.

Sometimes the offer of assistance mentioned in the last few lines of the letter seems a little weak, especially after the threatening news that preceded it. But it's typical for colleges to take a stance of challenge and support: Show us that you're interested in meeting our rigorous standards, and we'll do everything we can to help you be successful. After all, it's not acceptable behavior for advisers and counselors to haul you off the campus sidewalk and into their offices. So you have to be the one to take the initiative, follow-up the invitation, and show signs of wanting help.

Your college believes it sets the stage for change by letting you know that your academic situation is in jeopardy and that there are certain criteria you must meet in order to continue at the college. To support your efforts, the college provides campus resources that it hopes you will decide to use. That's the message, in a nutshell, that your college sent to you in your probation letter.

And what do you do if your probation letter continues to trigger visions of failure that discourage and depress you? Consider the reply of Benjamin Barber, political science professor at Rutgers University, when he was asked to react to our cultural tendency to label people as either successes or failures.[1]

> I don't divide the world into the weak and the strong, or the successes and failures, those who make it or those who don't. . . . I divide the world into learners and nonlearners.
>
> There are people who learn, who are open to what happens around them, who listen, who hear the lessons. When they do something stupid, they don't do it again. And when they do something that works a little bit, they do it even better and harder the next time.
>
> The question to ask is not whether you are a success or a failure, but whether you are a learner or a nonlearner.*

Your probationary letter delivers the message that you are not meeting your college's academic standards. If you are a nonlearner, you're stuck with this news and you put all your time and energy into judging yourself and your past. If you are a learner, you listen to the message and hear what it says to you. You've received an invitation to improve, and because you're a learner, you openly consider how to accept it.

Looking in the Mirror

Check over the letter from your college and figure out the conditions of your probation. If it's difficult to get this information from your letter, contact your college advisor; it is important for you to know exactly what you need to do. Then fill in the information below.

To meet the conditions of my college probation, I must

- complete _____ credits this term.

- earn a grade of _____ in each course or an overall GPA of _____ for the term.

- schedule a meeting to discuss my probationary status with my adviser or _____ by _____ .

- make an appointment to meet with a learning skills, financial aid, personal, or career counselor or _____ to discuss my situation by _____ .

*From When Smart People Fail *by C. Hyatt and L. Gottlieb, 1987, p. 233. Copyright ©* 1987 *by Penguin Books. Reprinted by permission.*

In addition to meeting these conditions, the letter says I need to _____

_____

_____

_____

_____

_____

_____

_____

_____

I personally would also like to _____

_____

_____

_____

_____

_____

_____

_____

_____

If I do not meet the probationary conditions set by the college this term, I realize that there are direct consequences. In the short term, these consequences are that I _____

_____

_____

_____

_____

_____

_____

_____

Longer term consequences could include _____

_____

_____

4

Breaking the Silence

Failure is not a popular topic. When people don't succeed, they usually feel that they have done something wrong. They react to failure by feeling ashamed that they didn't try harder or angry that they put themselves in an impossible situation in the first place. Sometimes they wish that circumstances had been different. They find themselves thinking "I should have studied more" or "I wish I'd taken a lighter course load" or "If only I hadn't worked so many hours to pay for my tuition and expenses." Do you ever find yourself thinking this way?

As typical as such responses are, there are other ways to look at failure. Rather than beat yourself up because things are not what you'd like them to be, you might remind yourself that learning means taking chances and growth involves risk. Trying something new means exposing yourself to the possibility of failure. You might find that learning calculus in college is unlike anything you've done in math before. You might feel foolish as you take part in a presentation in front of the class, away from the safety of a back-row seat. You might make mistakes. You might not know exactly how to get what you want. In short, you're moving into new territory. You're not sure exactly what the outcome will be.

Imagine what it could be like if people looked at failure differently. Would it be easier to risk failing if everyone viewed failure as a necessary link to growth and success? Would parents cheer (or at least approve) when students took intelligent risks? Would friends support each other in exploring new areas of interest? What if people talked like this:

"John has never studied Russian before," his father said, "but he is so interested in international exchange that he decided to give it a try; he's going to repeat the first level again this term and see how much progress he can make. We told him not to worry about the cost of repeating Russian I—learning a new language is worth a few extra dollars!"

"Did you hear that my friend Sue has decided to expand on her engineering background and try some courses in the humanities? She's not certain what her grades will be, but she's excited about getting involved in the liberal arts. Sounds risky but fun—maybe I should join her!"

What if our failures led us to join the ranks of Tolstoy (who flunked out of college), Edison (whose teachers told him he was too stupid to learn), and Beethoven (whose teacher told him he was hopeless as a composer)? Or if we ended up like Louis Pasteur (rated mediocre in college chemistry), Winston Churchill (failed at the sixth-grade level), or Walt Disney (fired for having "no good ideas")?[2] Not bad company!

In their book *When Smart People Fail*, Carole Hyatt and Linda Gottlieb[3] show how the field of science tends to regard failure in a positive light. When the authors asked one scientist how he has the energy to continue his attempts to cure diabetes through transplant technology when he has experienced nothing but failure for years, he replied, "I never think of what I do as failure. It's just an incomplete result. I always have in my mind what I am trying to accomplish, and each experiment tells me a little more about what I have done wrong."*

*From *When Smart People Fail* by C. Hyatt and L. Gottlieb, 1987, p. 36. Copyright © 1987 by Penguin Books. Reprinted by permission.

Learning through error may not be the easiest path to take, but it is a familiar one to many successful people. One graduating college senior told his family about his experience:

"I found out the hard way that succeeding in college requires more than memorizing molecular structures and analyzing philosophical arguments. I had to learn to anticipate what mix of classes would make a balanced course load for me and to know when to yell 'help!' or hire a tutor. Just accepting what came my way and hoping for the best during my first year almost ended in disaster. But when I started using what I found out one term to plan my approach for the next, then I made progress."

If you are willing, you can learn from your errors. Like the scientist and the college student, you need to fix in your mind what you want to accomplish and use the information you gain along the way to make adjustments. What score do you earn on your biology exam when you attend all of the labs but only half of the lectures? How well do you understand the presentation in your calculus class when you spend 15 minutes each day working sample problems? Does the lecture make more sense when you work problems with a friend for 60 minutes? Does it improve your theme for composition class when you allow time for revision, or do you write just as well at the last minute? How much rehearsal does it take to give a good presentation in your speech class? Different students get different results from similar efforts, so it's important to be aware of what works for you.

The road that links failure to success requires finding the connection between what you do and the results you get. When you're not getting the results you want, change is in order. It makes sense to take a look at what's happening and consider what you might do differently. Not everyone can do this. People who let failure intimidate them, in fact, find it just about impossible. Stewart Emery, author of *Actualizations,* tells about his experience with failure:

> Failure, for the most part, is not a result of our lack of ability but a product of our basic lack of observation of the yellow and red alerts that pop up in life. . . . I see that most people don't make the necessary correction, because they are too busy being concerned with protection. Most people's failures in life are a product of protecting themselves when they should have been correcting themselves.

> The unwillingness to be in error and correct is the source of most failures. Successful people . . . are willing to be in error and they are willing to correct. They are people who are busily doing what they don't know for sure how to do. That's the adventure for them. They don't know what's around the next corner. All they know is that they are committed to the path and they will do whatever has to be done.[4]

Students committed to earning a college degree watch for the "yellow and red alerts that pop up" and consider what options might move them closer to their goal of graduation. Would working with a tutor in the writing lab improve the quality of that history paper due next week? Would joining a study group in psychology put those detailed research studies in perspective? What would happen if you met students from your language class and spoke Spanish during lunch each day?

Students who are primarily interested in protecting themselves, on the other hand, use their energy to deny or defend their failure. Rather than correcting their course, these students set out to prove that failure is an inevitable result of their circumstances.

Sometimes this protection starts early in the term. Results from the first quiz feed the rumor that "Professor Smith gives terrible tests." By the time the midterm arrives, talk in the hallway centers on "Why waste time getting ready for an unfair exam?" Then, when grades at the end of the term confirm their failure, the students use the "impossible" situation in Professor Smith's class to protect their self-image. Students who want to defend their failure argue that given the circumstances, it was all right to fail. Students who protect themselves through denial, on the other hand, conclude that it was Professor Smith who failed—not them.

Yet what would have happened if these students had been willing to be in error and had tried a little correction instead of protection? What if they had discussed with Professor Smith the best way to prepare for an upcoming exam, or if they had contacted some successful students from Professor Smith's class of the previous term and found out what they did to learn the course material?

Being "in error" is uncomfortable because we're not sure how to correct our course, and there are no guarantees that the next thing we try will lead to improvement. But breaking the silence on failure reduces its power. When you admit that you goofed, you stop protecting yourself. Accepting the reality of probation, you open yourself to possibilities that can improve your situation. Then you can consider your options and correct your course for the next stretch of the journey.

Lots of times when we try something new, we initially get less than spectacular results. Remember your first dive off the high board at the neighborhood pool? Or when you first tried to parallel park your family car? We make mistakes, then learn how to correct our errors—and ultimately go on to accomplish our intended goal.

Whether it's learning to ride a bike or learning to excel in college, the process is the same. When have you been through this process before?

I wasn't successful when I first tried to _____

_____

_____

_____

_____

_____

_____

_____

_____

_____

My first attempts resulted in _____

_____

_____

_____

_____

_____

_____

_____

_____

_____

I decided that if I was going to be successful at this, I would have to

_____

_____

_____

_____

_____

_____

_____

_____

_____

I can use this experience to help me _____

_____

_____

_____

_____

_____

_____

_____

_____

5

Figuring Out What Went Wrong

To learn from error, you have to take a close look at what went wrong. Having accepted the fact that you're on probation, you switch your energy from dealing with the news of probation to figuring out what you can do to get different results. But before it's possible to decide what will work, it's helpful to figure out what did not.

Analyzing what went wrong is no easy chore. Some students have a strong urge to shout "Everything!" Others just as adamantly reply "Nothing!" But learning in college is a complex task. You have immense freedom, which means that choices are everywhere. What courses should you take? Which ones look interesting, and which ones do you have the right background for? How should you study? What is important to learning for each course, and what will you expect to do with what you learn? In addition to all this, how do you balance what you want personally with what the college expects of you?

What makes college learning difficult? Since your situation is unique to you, you may find that no one else's answer to that question exactly fits your circumstances. Try using the ideas on the following pages to spur your thinking, letting them guide you toward some conclusions about your own situation.

Learning in College Is Difficult When . . .

☑ personal factors interfere with your performance.

☑ you're unhappy with the institution you're attending.

☑ you have problems with your courses.

☑ your approach to studying does not bring good results.

☑ you're not really sure that you want to be in college.

Let's consider these ideas one at a time.

Learning in College Is Difficult When Personal Factors Interfere with Your Performance

Students report that what's going on in their personal lives has a tremendous impact on both their motivation to study and their ability to learn effectively.

"All I could think about was my boyfriend and how much we were fighting. I'd open my chemistry book and I'd think 'Should I call him?' I knew that worrying about our relationship was hurting my grades, but I just couldn't concentrate on anything else."

"I'd sit in the back of my history lecture and think about my lack of money. I knew I had enough to get through winter quarter, but what would I do in the spring? I'd take a few notes, and then the same old questions would pop up again. How are you going to pay for next quarter? Can you really afford to be in college?"

"I was always sick. Every time I sat down to study, my body reminded me how awful I felt. I'd tell myself to go to class and keep up with assignments, but I was working through a fog. I felt discouraged all the time, and I just wanted to sleep."

What Personal Issues Have Interfered with Your Performance?

On the next page, mark an item with a "✓" if it has been somewhat of a problem for you and with a "✓✓" if it has interfered with your progress on a regular basis. List additional issues at the end of the chart.

_____ poor health	_____ family problems
_____ financial difficulty	_____ social distractions
_____ too many commitments	_____ change in relationship with someone important to you
_____ unresolved problems	
_____ lack of confidence in your abilities	_____ anxiety
_____ clash between job and school	_____ loneliness
_____ other personal issues (list)	

_____   _____

_____   _____

_____   _____

Learning in College Is Difficult When You're Unhappy with the Institution You're Attending

Once you're at a college, you find out more about what it's really like. When your everyday campus experience is far different from what you would like it to be, you may find it harder to achieve the results you want.

"No one here seems to be interested in teaching students. The faculty teach their classes, then disappear from campus."

"I can't seem to get accurate information. One adviser tells me I have to do things one way, then I talk to someone else and the story changes."

"The students aren't at all what I expected. Everyone is very competitive, and no one seems willing to talk. I wish people would be friendlier."

What Institutional Factors Have Made Learning Difficult for You?

Mark an item with a "✓" if it has been somewhat of a problem and with a "✓✓" if it has interfered with your progress on a regular basis. List additional issues at the end of the chart.

_____ poor advising

_____ poor teaching

_____ problems with an instructor

_____ classes too large or too small

_____ inconvenient hours

_____ no interest in your needs as a learner

_____ campus values differ from yours

_____ other institutional factors (list)

_____ lack of good tutors

_____ inadequate facilities for studying

_____ few support services to help students with problems

_____ no opportunity for involvement with other students

_____ few people with backgrounds and interests like yours

_____   _____

_____   _____

_____   _____

Learning in College Is Difficult When You Have Problems with Your Courses

The particular courses you choose as well as your overall course load and schedule for a given term may influence your success.

"I enrolled in a math class and within days knew that the course was over my head. I supposedly had the right prerequisites, so I stayed in and hoped that I could make a decent grade. But my background just wasn't strong enough for me to keep up with the pace of the class."

"My GPA took a nose dive because I tried to do too much. My credit load looked fine on paper, but two of my classes had labs. I short changed my other courses in order to get everything done for the labs. Unfortunately, at the end of the term I paid a price for that choice."

"I couldn't motivate myself to study for my history and economics courses. What did they have to do with a career in music? So I turned what should have been study time for history and economics into extra practice sessions in the music hall. I fooled myself into believing I was making progress toward my degree until I saw my transcript for the term."

What Course Problems Have Made Learning Difficult for You?

Mark an item with a "✓" if it has been somewhat of a problem and with a "✓✓" if it has interfered with your progress on a regular basis. List additional issues at the end of the chart.

_____ no interest in a particular course

_____ inappropriate background for a course

_____ course load too heavy

_____ uncertain about your academic and career goals

_____ course does not fit your academic and career goals

_____ no tutors or other support for course

_____ other course problems (list)

_____ burnout from taking classes

_____ unrealistic choice of courses

_____ courses unavailable when you need them

_____ unrealistic amount of work assigned in courses

_____ too little time available in your schedule to complete the coursework

_____   _____

_____   _____

_____   _____

Learning in College Is Difficult When Your Approach
to Study Does Not Bring Good Results

Many people don't realize that there are different ways to go about studying. Yet how you study can make a tremendous difference in how well you learn. Your approach has an impact on the quality of your work as well as on your performance in classroom and test situations.

"I used to study in spurts. As a deadline got close, I'd read my textbooks for hours. Or I'd stay up all night to cram for a test or write a paper. Then I'd back off for a week or so to recover, storing up energy for my next marathon."

"I scheduled enough time to study, but I never knew exactly what I should be doing to get ready for a test. Which was more important, my classroom notes or the textbook reading? And all those details— which of them would I need to know?"

"Getting ready for a test for me meant getting all the material onto one chart, and then studying the chart until I knew it perfectly. When the system worked, I felt fantastic. A lot of the time though, I didn't end up with the grade I wanted. But I didn't know what else to do."

Has Your Approach to Studying Hindered
Your Academic Progress?

Mark an item with a "✓" if it has been somewhat of a problem and with a "✓✓" if it has interfered with your progress on a regular basis. List additional issues at the end of the chart.

_____ good intentions but poor follow-through

_____ concentration easily broken

_____ worries about failure interrupt thinking

_____ spotty reading of textbooks

_____ unprepared for classes

_____ unexpected questions on tests

_____ lecture notes useless for studying

_____ unsure about how to learn material

_____ uncertain about what is important

_____ too little time for review

_____ material quickly forgotten

_____ memorization substituted for understanding

_____ too little time to prepare for tests

_____ other approaches to studying (list)

_____   _____

_____   _____

_____   _____

Learning in College Is Difficult When You're Not Really Sure That You Want to Be in College

Students who question their commitment to college often feel unmotivated to do the everyday work that earning a degree in higher education requires.

"I sit down to study, and immediately I start daydreaming about places I'd rather be or things I'd rather be doing. I make myself read my sociology book, but my heart's not in it."

"Everyone in my family went straight from high school to college. I kept up the tradition, but after the first term I knew that staying in school was going to be tough. It's hard for me to keep going through the motions of being a student. I'm tired of this routine."

"I'm balancing a 30-hour-per-week job with being a full-time student. By the time I get through work and classes, I'm not in much of a mood to study. Basically, I like my job and my classes. But I can't keep up, and choosing between work and school is no easy decision."

How Right Is College for You at This Point in Your Life? Which of The Following Factors Make Learning Difficult?

Mark an item with a "✓" if it has been somewhat of a problem and with a "✓✓" if it has interfered with your progress on a regular basis. List additional issues at the end of the chart.

_____ enrolled in college only because you were expected to

_____ off-campus activities distract you

_____ self-discipline rather than motivation keeps you on campus

_____ life seems to be "on hold"

_____ prefer job responsibilities to schoolwork

_____ little interest in courses

_____ unsure how college fits into your goals

_____ energy low for completing assignments

_____ other motivational problems (list)

_____ learning is rarely fun

_____ negative emotions (stress, boredom) part of college routine

_____   _____

_____   _____

_____   _____

Looking in the Mirror

As you check over your lists of what has made learning in college difficult, pick out the factors that seem to have made the most difference to you as a learner. Use these factors to help figure out what's been going wrong for you as a college student.

Learning in college is difficult for me when _____

_____

_____

_____

_____

_____

_____

_____

In considering what's been going wrong for me in college, then, I realize that I need to take a look at how I can work on _____

_____

_____

_____

_____

_____

_____

_____

_____

6

Talking about Probation

You've put some energy into figuring out what's been going wrong for you in college, and you're just about ready to go out and turn things around. But before you jump into action, take a minute to pull together your ideas.

In itself, being on probation is a pretty straightforward state of affairs—when your college totaled up the number of credits you attempted and reviewed your results for the term, you came up short. Your thoughts and feelings about probation, however, tend to be more complex, and can make it very difficult to figure out what to tell other people about your academic status. What do you say to your parents? How do you respond to your friends' questions about how you did last term?

Telling people about probation is tricky because the way you interpret what happened has an impact on what you feel capable of doing. If you say that you failed at being a student last term, your own interpretation of your probationary status may leave you feeling defeated. You find yourself involved again and again in conversations that dwell on what went wrong. By the time you repeat the details to several people, you feel depressed, which just compounds the problem. Your energy for starting another term slowly drains away as part of your mind worries about what will happen next.

Career consultants Carole Hyatt and Linda Gottlieb, who counsel people who have been fired or laid off from their jobs, have discovered that people can benefit when they reinterpret events.[5]

> Reinterpreting your past to put it in the most positive light is simply good mental health. There is no 'objective' truth to what happened. All stories are told through a narrator and in this case you are both narrator and audience. If as narrator you constantly tell yourself a negative story, you as audience feel sad and powerless. If as narrator you downplay the negative events and emphasize the hero's accomplishments, you as audience are likely to be inspired. The events have not changed, only the narration. A sports coach whose team is losing in the first half could say to his team at halftime, "You guys really messed up in there, and we're in deep trouble"; or the coach could reinterpret the same facts and say, "Even though we are behind, we have plenty of time to catch up and win." One statement emphasizes past defeats; the other acknowledges past defeats but concentrates on future victories.*

When people emphasize the negative, they feel like victims. They can't seem to do anything right, and whatever they do seems to make little difference. A positive interpretation of events, on the other hand, gives you energy to move ahead. You're taking control, and you're looking for ways to improve your situation.

Remember reading in Chapter 1 about Sara's reaction to probation? She was angry, and she felt that the system was to blame for her poor performance. Sara often talked about the unfairness of her situation with her family and friends:

"Being on probation puts all the pressure on me. I'm the one who has to shape up and make the grade. But it's these instructors who really need to take a look at what they're doing. They drone on and on, and don't even seem to notice whether or not students understand the material. They just walk to the front of the room, dictate pages of notes, and then pack their briefcases and leave. Instructors expect us to do well on tests, but they're not teaching us anything. I should just skip class and save myself the pain of sitting through a boring lecture."

Sara's parents and friends responded to her interpretation by trying to argue her out of her despair. "Ask your teachers questions," her parents would say. "Break the monotony of the lecture; get a discussion going!" Friends advised Sara to make a change: "Look around and find someone who's a better teacher, or drop the class and take it another term." Convinced that teaching in her college was not what it should be, Sara found it easy to dismiss their suggestions.

Let's look at a possible reinterpretation of Sara's circumstances. How might this way of telling the story change Sara's view of probation? How might it make a difference in how family and friends respond to Sara?

"I'm feeling a lot of pressure to do well because I'm on probation. My grades are low because my classes are difficult, and I really need some good teaching to help me understand the material. Last term I had some disappointing instructors, and I learned that counting on them to help me learn the material just didn't work out. So this time around I've formed a study group with some of my classmates. We teach each other, and when we get stuck we prepare a list of questions to ask the instructor. Our instructor lets us give her the questions before class begins, and she uses them to clear up any misunderstanding from the previous lesson. This makes the class a lot more interesting to me, and I definitely understand the material better."

How you talk about probation not only affects your approach to a new term, but it also shapes the reactions of people around you. Your friends, family, advisers, and instructors respond to the cues you give. Your situation remains the same: you're on probation for the term. But your attitude about yourself and what you hope to make happen during the next few weeks can make a big difference in the support you get.

Looking in the Mirror

What is the statement that you want to make about being on probation? How can you reinterpret this event so that the telling of your story not only describes your circumstances but also shows that you're taking control and looking for ways to improve your situation? As you prepare your statement, keep in mind that you want to respond to requests about your academic status in a way that

- acknowledges your current academic difficulty

- respects your worth as an individual

- focuses on what is ahead

- invites support for what you're doing

- gives you energy to do the things that will contribute to your academic success

I know you're wondering about how I did last term, and I want you to

know that _____

_____

_____

_____

_____

_____

_____

_____

_____

_____

I plan to _____

_____

_____

_____

_____

_____

_____

_____

_____

I hope that _____

_____

_____

_____

_____

_____

_____

_____

**PART
TWO**

**Taking Charge
of the Future**

7

Making the Transition

Many students hope that just their urge to "do better" will propel them from probation to success. College students across the nation who are disappointed with their grades sound the battle cry of "I'll try harder!" as a new term begins. With spiral notebooks and sharpened pencils in hand, they march off to classes determined that this will be their best term ever.

Unfortunately, few of these students get the results they want. Enthusiasm runs low by the end of the first few weeks as reality sets in. Stunned by their impending doom, they wonder why "trying harder" didn't bring success.

What many don't realize is that doing better often requires more than gritting your teeth and digging in your heels. The best of intentions can fall flat when your remedy for academic probation doesn't really address the problem. Here's what two students found when they first attempted to improve their academic status:

"I couldn't figure out why I wasn't doing better. I failed trig the term before, so I jumped right back in and enrolled in the class a second

time. I thought sitting through the class again would guarantee my success. But when I got my midterm grade, I found myself staring at an 'F' again."

"I decided that attending classes would help me raise my GPA, so I scheduled all my courses on Monday, Wednesday, and Friday to make it easier for me to get to campus. That worked for two weeks. But when I started getting behind, I cut class to work on my assignments. Once I skipped my first class, it didn't make sense to drive in to attend the others. Pretty soon I was missing just as many classes as I had the semester before."

Motivation counts for a lot, but it doesn't take care of everything. Repeating an experience that didn't work the first time won't necessarily turn out better the second time around simply because you're willing to try again. If your background for the course is inadequate, you'll need to fill in the gaps to get yourself ready to start at the same level with the rest of the class. If being exposed to the course content isn't enough to ensure that you'll understand it, you'll need to find a way to make sense of the material you need to learn. If skipping classes has significantly interfered with your progress in the past, then you've learned a self-defeating habit that took some time to develop—and that now is going to take some effort to break.

Doing better in college usually involves changing how you go about being a student. Even though your approach to learning may have worked for you in the past, your probationary status tells you that it's not working now. Changing your approach will require some careful thinking about what you do, since people are creatures of habit and feel most comfortable when they do things in the same old way—even when the old way doesn't work.

Change can be difficult. You're making a transition from one way of doing things to another, and old habits of thinking and acting may not easily give way to the new. According to William Bridges, writer and lecturer on human development, there are three phases to any transition and you'll probably go through them as you change to a new approach to college success. You'll experience an ending, followed by a period of confusion and distress, leading to a new beginning.[6] Let's look at this process in terms of a student on probation.

1. Every Transition Begins with an Ending

Your first response to this might be "Great! I'm ready for something different!" But as you say goodbye to probation, what else will you be leaving? Here's what some students in your situation had to say:

"I wondered what my life would be like if I became a 'good' student. Would I have to study all the time? Could I keep my part-time job? Would I still have a chance to do the things that are important to me, like skiing on weekends or hiking in the mountains?"

"I was a member of a fraternity, and I had to improve my grades if I wanted to stay active. I realized that I wanted the best of all worlds— you know, go out with the guys every night and still have great grades. But that's not how it worked for me. And I worried that if I dropped out of the party scene to give myself more time to study, I might lose my friends. Somehow good grades and no friends didn't seem like much of a deal to me."

As you think about making changes to improve your grades, think about what things might have to stop. Like the students above, do you worry about how a commitment to doing better in college might affect your lifestyle? Will you have to spend your time differently than before? On the other hand, will you be glad to say "goodbye" to some of the negatives that go along with academic difficulty? Will a change in approach to college reduce some of the stress you've been under?

Being as specific as possible, list below some of the "endings" that may be part of your transition from probation to academic success. Write a "+" next to the items that you see as easy to let go and a "−" next to the items that might be hard to give up.

**Moving from Probation to Academic Success
May Mean Saying Goodbye to:**

Example:

__−__ lots of free time   __+__ worrying about grades

____ _____   ____ _____

____ _____   ____ _____

___   _____   ___   _____

___   _____   ___   _____

___   _____   ___   _____

Most people find endings difficult, even when they believe they are moving on to something better. It's hard to just walk away and say "That's it, this style of living doesn't work for me anymore." You might even want to give some additional thought to the items with a "−" next to them, since they represent areas that have some "pull" for you. Though you may feel strongly that doing well in college means giving up something that you would like to keep, you may also find it's possible to modify rather than completely discard it. Here's one student who did some negotiating to make his life more tolerable:

"When I got on probation, I realized my parents had been paying thousands of dollars a year to my college for my social life. I knew the first thing that had to go was my 'fun.' I threw myself into academics and said 'no' to my friends: no more socializing in the student union, no more parties. All that would have to wait until another semester.

It wasn't long before this new routine felt like prison. I could make myself sit down and study, but I couldn't make myself concentrate. I needed to be around people—not only because they're fun, but because they give me energy and make life seem worthwhile. So I worked out a compromise. When I studied a certain number of hours each day, I rewarded myself with time with my friends. When I finished a major paper or a project, I celebrated with a friend. My new system helped me do better in school, and I actually enjoyed the time I spend with my friends more because I didn't have to feel guilty about being away from the books."

So before you go "cold turkey" with your endings, think about what you're letting go. At least for right now, say "goodbye" to the ways of thinking and acting that definitely interfere with your success. Work for balance with the others, knowing that your goal is to be the one in control. You want to be in charge of your life rather than let your habits control you. As you let go of your old approach to being a student, you're negotiating a new and better way of doing things.

Remember, every transition begins with an ending. With an eye toward your college degree, choose what you want to leave behind. Regrets are understandable—some lifestyles just aren't compatible with a good GPA!

2. The Second Stage of Transition, the "Neutral Zone," Is a Period of Reorientation

The neutral zone in your transition can feel pretty uncomfortable. You're aware that you want to change, and you're trying to leave behind habits that you know don't work for you. You may feel like you're in limbo, disconnected from the past and not yet on the way toward your future. You look for advice about what to do next, and no one seems to have any answers. Here's how one student described her experience in the neutral zone:

"I remember that my first week of classes as a probationary student was terrible. I knew I had to do better than I had the previous quarter, but I didn't know how. I talked with my adviser about what to do to improve, and she really didn't tell me anything definite. Nothing felt certain anymore. I wanted advice—something that would turn my life around if I would just make myself do it. But no one would tell me what to do."

As frustrating as this part of the transition is, it can be the time when you figure out what's important to you and how to get what you really want. You're in the process of reorienting yourself, and no one can do that for you. Some students react by getting angry that people aren't more helpful, while others feel let down or lonely. One student said that realizing there's no universal key to college success was much like finding out the truth about Santa Claus, the Easter Bunny, and the Tooth Fairy!

Realize that what you are noticing is the gap between who you were as a student and the student you want to become. You're open to change, and part of you wishes that raising your hand and volunteering to be a successful student would finalize the deal. But easy as it is to be disenchanted when no one gives you their private copy of *The Secret To College Success*, remember that you are working through an important part of the transition process. You are preparing yourself for a new beginning, a beginning that's right for you in particular.

3. When You're Ready, You'll Find the Opportunities You Need to Make a New Beginning

You've made your endings. You've stumbled through the neutral zone, searching for the procedures manual that tells you how to shape up your student experience in ten easy steps. You've talked with friends, parents, advisers, and anyone else who would listen to you. Tinkering with doing things a little differently than you have in the past, you stop and wonder: Is this my new beginning? Have I found my secret to success? Am I making any progress toward getting off probation and on with my education?

New beginnings are often unimpressive; sometimes they even start without announcing themselves. They may pop up in the form of an idea, or you may intuitively feel drawn to doing something a certain way. One college sophomore describes her new beginning like this:

"When I first got on probation, I was really angry that people didn't seem to want to help me more. Advisers would say things like "Watch the kinds of courses you take" or "Don't load yourself down with too many credit hours." My parents said "Do your best and things will work out." Friends were friends, telling me that I was a smart person and not to worry about probation too much. I guess people thought they were being supportive, but I thought their answers were too glib. It felt like they weren't taking my problem seriously.

I started off the new term, conscious of everything I did and didn't do. Of course I worked hard, and I kept talking to students in my classes about how they were learning the material. I even made an appointment with the instructor of my toughest class to see if I was on the right track with one of the written assignments. But still I was afraid. Were these changes going to be enough?

One day as I was walking across campus, it struck me: college is hard for everybody. This idea really hit me—not in a way that

discouraged me, but in a way that almost excited me. The realiza-
tion that everyone has to figure out how to cope with the demands
of college was a new beginning for me. Rather than just waiting to
find out if my work was up to par, I needed to figure out how to
learn in each of my classes.

It seems trite to say that I woke up to what college learning in-
volves, but I think that's what happened. I had to let go of what I
thought college would be like, and I had to be OK with the fact that
successful college students do things differently than successful high
school students. Once I got this new image in my head, I knew I was
right on track."

Like this student, your new beginning will also rise out of the muck
of confusion that's a natural part of any transition. Listen to the signals
that point to your new beginnings—the thoughts that return to nag
you, the ideas that say "Pay attention to me; I want to tell you something."

When you're really ready for a change, you will find a beginning
that's right for you. Your beginning will give you the energy to form
and carry out a plan that will take you from probation to academic
success. Your plan will keep you aware of what you're doing, as well
as guide you in the direction that you want to go. And because it's
yours, the plan will work.

In the next chapter, we look at putting together your plan in
greater detail. But before moving on, give some thought to where you
are in terms of the three stages of transition.

Using William Bridges's ideas[7] on the three stages of transition as
springboards for your thinking, take a look at where you are in the
process of changing from a student on probation to a student successfully completing a degree at your college. Respond to each of the following quotations in terms of your own situation.

Stage 1:

"Every transition begins with an ending. We have to let go of the
old thing before we can pick up the new—not just outwardly, but

inwardly, where we keep our connections to the people and places that act as definitions of who we are." *

What endings are part of your transition to academic success?

As a student on probation who wants to successfully complete a college degree, I realize that the most significant thing I am leaving be-

hind is _____

_____

_____

_____

_____

_____

_____

_____

_____

_____

_____

_____

_____

William Bridges, Transitions, © 1980, by Addison-Wesley Publishing Company, Inc. Reprinted with permission of the publisher.

Stage 2:

"The second hurdle of transition is a seemingly unproductive time-out when we feel disconnected from people and things in the past and emotionally unconnected to the present. Yet the Neutral Zone is really a time of reorientation . . . it is the phase of the transition process that the modern world pays least attention to. Treating ourselves like appliances that can be unplugged and plugged in again at will or cars that stop and start with the twist of a key, we've forgotten the importance of fallow time."*

How are you dealing with this in-between stage, in which you've left behind your old way of being a student and haven't yet found a new one?

As I sort out what's happening and reorient myself toward being a successful student in this college, I find that this part of the transition is

_____

_____

_____

_____

_____

_____

_____

_____

_____

*William Bridges,Transitions, © 1980, by Addison-Wesley Publishing Company, Inc. Reprinted with permission of the publisher.

Stage 3:

"In transitions we come to beginnings only at the end, when we launch new activities. To make a successful New Beginning requires more than simply persevering. It requires an understanding of external signs and inner signals that point the way to the future."*

What external signs and inner signals are pointing the way to your future? What understanding have you gained about moving from probation to academic success?

As a student who is interested in earning a college degree, my new

beginning involves _____

_____

_____

_____

_____

_____

_____

_____

_____

_____

**William Bridges, Transitions, © 1980, by Addison-Wesley Publishing Company, Inc. Reprinted with permission of the publisher.*

8

Devising a Plan

Any student can fantasize about doing better or getting good grades. But achievers do more than just dream of college success—they make it happen.

Picture yourself on the way to a final exam, confident that you're ready to answer any question. As you walk across campus, you mentally review the course's key concepts one more time. You're aware that you know the material well and that you feel good about the upcoming exam. The test will be a good chance to show what you've learned.

A ring of the telephone brings you back to the present, and you chuckle as you note the disparity between your daydream and what really happened at the end of last term. Preparing for finals then consisted of worrying about what the test questions would be and whether or not you would be able to answer them. Since you understood only part of the course content in chemistry and were behind in history, geography, and literature, you never even got to cover all the material you needed to learn.

If you're an achiever, you'll use your daydream. Rather than just dismissing your pictures of what you would like your student experience to be, you'll use them to create what you want. The very contrast between where you are today and what you want to be in the future can help you make decisions that support your achievement. If you want final exam week to be different this semester, you'll figure out what you need to do on a daily basis throughout the term to make that happen. To reduce the anxiety you associate with learning, you'll take steps to get it under control. You know that if you want to turn your wishes into reality, you need to make a plan and follow it.

A good plan requires your involvement. You know better than anyone else what will guide you over the rough spots and help you make the everyday decisions that are critical to your success. Using the following guidelines to trigger your thinking, start making your own plan for getting off probation and on with your education. Here are the basic steps.

1. Define what you want.

2. Decide how much you want it.

3. Take charge.

Let's look at these one at a time.

1. Define What You Want

Figuring out exactly what you want from the college experience is the critical first step in devising your plan. You'll definitely increase your chances for getting what you want if you know what that is!

You can begin the process of defining what you want by stating a general long-term goal: I want to get my college degree. You then break this broad, overall goal into more specific academic, personal, and social goals:

I want to learn about the field of environmental issues.

I want to learn to think critically about difficult issues.

I want to take part in campus activities.

The goals reflect your own values and help you focus your energy on what's important to you.

Defining your goals also helps you discover what you can do to achieve them. When you know what you want, you find courses that intrigue you, issues that excite you, and people that you want to connect with. You're a student with a purpose, going somewhere.

Sometimes, however, discovering what you want from college is difficult. What should you choose for a major? Should you focus your study on an area you enjoy, or should you pick a field with good job potential? How important are grades? How much time can you spend on campus activities or a part-time job? If no one way of doing things seems right, it's easy to let all the possibilities stump you. And choosing doesn't get any easier when there are other people who would like to lead your life for you. Sometimes it's even tempting to let them, given the hassles that defining your own goals may involve.

Career coach and management consultant Adele Scheele, author of *Skills for Success,* tells people interested in career advancement that the world of working people is made up of Sustainers and Achievers.[8] These categories reflect people's beliefs about who they are, what they want, and who defines what they want.

The world of higher education is also made up of Sustainers and Achievers. Sustainers are students who may perform well enough to meet the academic requirements of their institution but who have little personal connection with their college experience. Often Sustainers are enrolled in college because someone expects them to be, and they passively carry out their student responsibilities. They get their assignments, complete the work, and hope their efforts will be acceptable. Sustainers wait for approval from their instructors and resign themselves to whatever the outcome might be. They feel relieved when they do well, and they briefly wonder what happened when they don't. Sustainers think the college experience is OK, but they basically feel they're putting in time until their "real life" begins. And if their college degree doesn't open the "right" doors immediately upon graduation, Sustainers resent their time spent in college.

Achievers approach college in a different way. They are in college because they believe it's the best place for them to be. Achievers actively think about what they want, and they look for ways to make it happen. When it comes to assignments, Achievers make sure they understand what the instructor is looking for—and they also think about what it is that they themselves want to learn. Achievers talk about their ideas, invite reactions from both instructors and friends, and work to understand why they get the feedback they do. Achievers do not always get the highest grades in the class, but their active involvement in learning makes most of their time in college enjoyable, and they're glad they're there.

Sustainers and Achievers both need to resolve the issue of who defines what they want from higher education, and they each make different decisions. Since Sustainers are not really in college for themselves, it seems natural when others make decisions about their learning for them. If invited to think about what they want, Sustainers often make excuses such as "I'm too busy to spend my time planning" or "Why worry about it? You either get lucky and get what you want, or you accept what comes your way." So Sustainers often let friends, parents, advisers, or instructors take control, even when they realize that this won't work well in the long run. Achievers, on the other hand, take responsibility for their own lives. They actively search for answers by talking with instructors, personal counselors, career experts, learning consultants, college advisers, and fellow students.

After looking around for advice, Achievers consider the possibilities that others have suggested. But they make the choices themselves. They decide what their majors will be, what courses they'll take, and how they will go about learning. They think about how they can balance their academic goals with what they want personally and socially during the time they're in college. In other words, Achievers define what they want from their college experience.

As you anticipate making your own plan, here are the questions you'll need to be thinking about:

- ☑ What do I want from the college experience?

- ☑ What are my academic goals?

- ☑ What are my personal goals?

- ☑ What are my social goals?

Your responses to these questions will form the basis of your plan for achievement.

2. Now That You've Defined What You Want, Decide How Much You Want It

How important is achieving each of your goals to you? How willing are you to carry out your plans?

It's one thing to think up a plan and another to carry it out, so it's important to be realistic about how much effort you're willing to devote to turning your wishes for college success into reality. Take a minute to look over these sample statements and see which category best reflects your commitment. How ready will you be to turn your goals into an action plan?

Low Commitment:

"I think these are good goals for someone in college to have."

"I'll try out my plan and see what happens, but I'm not expecting much. Plans work best for people who prefer structure, and I like to be able to respond to things as they come up."

Moderate Commitment:

"I can see how these goals could help keep me on track. I'll make a point of reviewing them once in a while to see how I'm doing."

"Writing my plan down on paper helped me realize that it's possible to get what I want from college. I hope I'll use the plan often enough to see some results this term."

High Commitment:

"I'm going to use these goals to keep my priorities straight. Whenever a choice comes up, I'm going to ask myself: Will doing this help me achieve one of my goals?"

"I'm going to *live* my plan this term! I'll review my goals each day and check on my progress each week."

It's important to realize that the results students get from working with their personal plan depends on the quality of their effort. If you are committed to finding a way to make your goals happen, you'll put your energy into figuring out how to turn your situation around and come out on top. If you put little or no thought into designing a plan that meets your own needs, the outcome of your efforts will be minimal. Even if you manage to come up with a gold star document that meets some expert's standards for planning, you'll be no further along in improving your situation if it doesn't fit you. So be realistic, and keep in mind who you are and what it is that you really want as you make up your plan. Then remember that the level of your commitment to carrying out your plan will shape the results you get.

Think about your answer to this question:

How committed am I to setting up and implementing a personal plan for college achievement?

Your response to this question will be a major factor in the success of your plan.

3. Take Charge

If you're committed to planning for your achievement, you're ready to get started. It's time to take charge and set up some workable short-term goals.

Clearly stated short-term goals give you something tangible to work on right now. "I want to earn a college degree" becomes "I want to earn a 'B' in calculus this quarter." You know that you're working on your long-term goal because doing well in calculus moves you one step closer to graduation. Yet you're concentrating on adding one piece at a time to the big picture.

You look at your short-term goal and think about how to break it down into specific tasks. You focus on what you need to do right now, today, and this week. What can you do now that will make a "B" in calculus possible for you?

Consider your alternatives. If you think you're weak in math, you might visit the math department or math learning center to see if they can help you find out if you really are. Do you have the background skills and knowledge you need to do well in the course? If not, what can you do to get them? If your background in math *is* OK, what can you do to support your learning in calculus once the course begins? Join a study group? Attend review sessions? Work with a tutor? In other words, you don't assume that simply enrolling in calculus will ensure that you will meet your short-term goal. Think about possible courses of action, and choose the tasks you believe will get you where you want to go. Together these tasks make up your action plan.

Let's take a look at how one student worked up an action plan. He decided on two long-term goals—earning a college degree and participating in his college's activities. Then he broke his broad goals into workable short-term goals and specific tasks.

Short-Term Goals and Tasks for Fall Term

Academic Goal 1:   *I want to earn a "B" in calculus this term.*

Tasks: I will study for a minimum of two hours outside class each day.

I will meet with the calculus study group immediately after class each day and review the lecture material and upcoming assignment.

I will earn at least a "B" on every assignment. When I am confused about what I'm trying to learn, I will meet with a tutor in the math lab.

Academic Goal 2:   *I want to attend all the classes for each course I'm enrolled in this term.*

Tasks: I will consider my attendance a required rather than a negotiable part of the course.

I will set two alarms to make sure that I get out of bed and start my class schedule each day.

I will make an attendance contract with one student in each of my classes.

Academic Goal 3:   *I want to find out how to deal with my test anxiety.*

Tasks: I will attend the workshop on test anxiety sponsored by the learning center.

I will make an appointment with a counselor to talk about my test anxiety last term.

Personal Goal 1:	*I want to join an exercise program and keep myself physically fit.*
Tasks:	I will call the campus recreation center to find out what exercise programs are available this term.
	I will join one of the exercise groups and work out one hour three times a week.
Personal Goal 2:	*I want to check into career options in the field of ecology.*
Tasks:	I will visit the career resource lab and look through the materials there.
	I will talk with my adviser about getting experience in ecology through a college internship.
Personal Goal 3:	*I want to be a student tutor for inner-city youth once a week.*
Tasks:	I will attend the tutor training session sponsored by the campus volunteer office.
	I will volunteer for a two-hour tutoring session one afternoon per week.
Social Goal 1:	*I want to join a student organization and take part in their activities this term.*
Tasks:	I will attend the introductory meeting for the bicycle club.
	I will go on two bicycle trips with the club.

Social Goal 2:	*I want to get to know at least two people in each of my classes.*
Tasks:	I will introduce myself to the students sitting next to me in my classes.
	I will exchange telephone numbers with students interested in working together.
Social Goal 3:	*I want to find out about campus-sponsored travel.*
Tasks:	I will call the campus travel office and ask them to send me a listing of trips available for spring break.

As you specify your goals and break them into specific tasks, check to see if they meet the following criteria:

Goal and Task Checklist

☑ Are these goals mine? Do they reflect what I really want?

☑ Did I state my goals and tasks in specific terms? Will I be able to tell when I have completed the tasks and achieved my goals?

☑ Have I been positive about what I intend to do? Have I stated what I will do rather than what I won't?

☑ Are my goals and tasks realistic given my personal skills and lifestyle?

Student goals and tasks that meet these standards have a good chance of success. Can you predict what will happen when students choose an approach that doesn't meet these standards? How helpful are the following goals and tasks?

- I will try not to fail this term.

- I will do my best in each of my courses.

- I will study all day, every day, and leave my socializing for another term.

- I won't disappoint my family and friends with my scholastic performance this term.

Obviously not just any goal or task can give you the direction and energy you need in order to improve. When goals are stated negatively, they focus your attention on what you are trying to avoid rather than direct your energy toward what you want to accomplish. When tasks are too general, it is difficult to know exactly what you should do during the next 24 hours to achieve them. If you can't tell when you've completed a goal or task, you won't know if you're making any progress. And if you're not working on your own goals, chances are you won't have enough commitment to follow through with your plan.

You want your goals and tasks to guide you as you move ahead, helping you decide the best way to use your time and energy each day. When you replace vague hopes of doing better with definite steps for accomplishing what you want, you're going to like the results you get. Take the time to direct your efforts with workable goals and specific tasks that fit your needs. As you devise your plan, keep this question in mind:

How can I break my goals down into specific tasks that will help me be successful in college this term?

Your response to this question will give you the specific steps you need to put your plan into action.

Begin your plan for getting what you want out of college by completing the statements below. Keep in mind that you want to balance academics with personal and social goals.

I have certain **long-term goals** that I would like to achieve during my

next few years in college. Specifically, I want to _____

_____

_____

_____

_____

_____

_____

_____

_____

_____

_____

These **long-term goals** are important to me because _____

_____

_____

_____

_____

_____

_____

_____

_____

Having a general idea of what you want for your future gives you a chance to progress toward your goals one step at a time. As you think about how this term in college fits into the big picture, you'll find that there are things you want to accomplish during the next several weeks. List your short-term goals for this college term below, choosing specific tasks to do that will help you achieve each goal.

Short-Term Goals for _____ **Term**
                           (summer, fall, winter, spring)

Academic Goal 1:   I want to _____

_____

_____

Tasks: _____

_____

_____

_____

_____

_____

_____

_____

Level of commitment
to goal: _____

Academic Goal 2:   I want to _____

_____

_____

Tasks: _____

_____

_____

_____

_____

_____

_____

_____

Level of commitment
to goal: _____

Academic Goal 3:   I want to _____

_____

_____

Tasks: _____

_____

_____

_____

_____

_____

Level of commitment
to goal: _____

Personal Goal 1:   I want to _____

_____

_____

Tasks: _____

_____

_____

_____

_____

_____

_____

Level of commitment
to goal: _____

Personal Goal 2:   I want to _____

_____

_____

Tasks: _____

_____

_____

_____

_____

_____

_____

_____

Level of commitment
to goal: _____

Personal Goal 3:   I want to _____

_____

_____

Tasks: _____

_____

_____

_____

_____

_____

Level of commitment
to goal: _____

Social Goal 1:   I want to _____

_____

_____

Tasks: _____

                              _____

                              _____

                              _____

                              _____

                              _____

                              _____

                              _____

Level of commitment
to goal: _____

Social Goal 2:   I want to _____

                              _____

                              _____

Tasks: _____

                              _____

                              _____

                              _____

                              _____

                              _____

                              _____

Level of commitment
to goal: _____

Social Goal 3:   I want to _____

_____

_____

Tasks: _____

_____

_____

_____

_____

_____

_____

Level of commitment
to goal: _____

Now that you have set up these goals and tasks, you've put together a plan that reflects what you want. Check to be sure that your goals and tasks are specific and that you've stated what you intend to do in positive terms.

Given your personal skills and lifestyle, how realistic does your plan look to you? How strong is your commitment to actually carrying out your plan?

As I get ready to put my plan into action, it's important for me to keep

in mind that _____

_____

_____

9

Implementing Your Plan

You've stated your goals and now have a course of action. It's a concrete plan for the next several weeks that you hope will get you off probation and on with your education. Now how do you get this plan off the paper and into your life?

Usually it involves three steps. You'll need to

1. select a day-to-day system that works.

2. pay attention to your thinking.

3. check your progress regularly.

Making decisions about how you want to go about each of these steps keeps you in control of your plan. Let's start with a look at your choices.

1. Select an Effective System of Structure and Support for Carrying Out Your Plan

You've set up short-term goals, and you've broken these goals down into specific tasks. Now what's this plan going to look like on a daily basis?

How you answer this question depends on your style of doing things. How much structure do you like? Are you comfortable with a time-oriented system that shows what you're going to do during each hour of the day, or are you more motivated by a task-oriented system that lists what you'll do but not when you'll do it? What kind of support do you want? Do you prefer to work alone, or with other people?

What's important is not what particular system you use, but that you find one that fits your personality. That's what will help you stay on track and complete the tasks that you've chosen for the next few weeks.

Here are some issues to consider as you think about the personalized structure and support that will enable you to get your plan off the ground.

☑   How will I prioritize what needs to be done? Which of the tasks on my list are the most important?

☑   How will I keep track of what I need to do? What will I do if I fall behind or run into difficulties?

☑   What if my motivation slips during the term and I don't feel like continuing my routine?

☑   When would it be helpful to connect with other people and resources to support my efforts?

Discussions by students who've worked their way off probation suggest some possibilities for you to consider:

Manuel: *"My roommate and I would each make a list of the tasks we needed to do for the next day. Then we'd read them off for the other to critique. Sometimes I'd get comments like 'That sounds possible' or 'That's probably OK if you're willing to work your tail off!' Other times I'd hear 'Get real!' and need to reconsider what I had in mind* *for the next 24 hours. Then we'd get together at the end of the fol-lowing day for a progress report. This worked well for me because it kept me thinking about what I was doing. And knowing I was going to check in with a friend helped me follow through with my plan."*

Tara: *"What worked for me was keeping an hourly schedule. First I wrote in all my routine commitments—my classes, my job, my weekly or-ganization meetings, and my commuting time. Then I looked to see what hours I had left, and scheduled different time slots for working on what I put down for my academic, personal, and social goals. I also kept a 'to do' list with my schedule—that way I knew what I specifically needed to do when I came to a time block that said 'Study history' or 'Study algebra.' I like this system because it not only let me know when I was going to work on my plan, but exactly what I would be doing."*

Amy: *"When I started working with my plan, I knew what I wanted to do. I had no trouble ranking my tasks, and I spaced my activities so that it looked like I had a pretty sane semester in front of me. My first weeks with the plan worked well, but then things started to fall apart.*

My study partner for French got sick and couldn't keep up her end of our review sessions. Then my literature professor moved the due date up one week for our theme paper. Just as I was juggling all these changes, I got a call from the campus library saying that the job I'd been hoping to get was now available.

Fortunately for me, I didn't follow my first instinct that said 'Throw out the plan!' Instead, I made an appointment with one of the consultants in the learning center, and we figured out some al-ternatives for me to try. The hardest thing for me to realize was that my plan was negotiable—there was more than one way to make it work. Before I talked with the learning consultant, I thought that my plan had to work that way or else not at all. I almost didn't give myself a chance!"

Your choices for a day-to-day system are limited only by your imagination. Do some thinking about the kind and amount of structure you work best with, then consider whether it would be useful to involve someone else in your plan. Is there a friend who you could check in with? A classmate who would also benefit from working with a plan? An adviser or learning consultant who would be willing to brainstorm with you if things get rocky? Anticipate what will make your plan work, and you'll have the structure and support for your success when you need it.

As you look ahead to implementing your plan, think about this question:

Knowing what I do about myself, what kind of structure and support will help me complete the tasks in my plan?

Your response to this question will help you figure out a way to make your plan workable for you.

2. Pay Attention to Your Thinking and Visualize Your Success

At last you're ready to use your plan for achievement! You've got goals, tasks, and a day-to-day system to help you get what you want.

Turning your plan into reality may feel a little awkward at first. After all, changing habits of thinking and acting is no easy matter. You may find yourself wondering, will doing all this make any difference? Will my plan to improve my situation in college actually work? Is success possible?

According to David Ellis, author of *Becoming a Master Student*,[9] such thinking suggests that it's time to yell "Stop!" Stop worrying whether you're doing what you should be doing to get off probation or whether you have the "right" plan for achievement. Just be the successful student that you want to be.

> Getting where you want to *be* by what you *do* or by what you *have* is like swimming against the current. It's much easier to go the other direction. To get what you want, *be* it.
>
> We usually work against nature by trying to *have* something or *do* something before *being* it. That's the hard way. All of your deeds (what you *do*) won't get you where you want to *be*. Getting all the right tools (what you *have*) won't get you there either.
>
> If you can visualize yourself where you want to be, if you can go there in your imagination, if you can be it, then you have achieved most of your goal. You will soon *have* and *do* what you want. This is true because, as human beings, we *subconsciously* create whomever we *think* we are. . . .

If you consider yourself stupid in math, you are likely to fail at math. If you are convinced that you have a poor memory, chances are that no matter how much you practice memory techniques, your memory won't improve much.

Great achievements happen as the result of very subtle actions that are often unconscious. If you want to succeed, reach to the source of those subconscious choices that determine your future. Do this by starting from *be*.

Starting from *be* doesn't guarantee anything; it is still necessary to use action to get what you want. But when you start from a mind-set of *being*, your actions become much more natural and on target. That's because your body is not fighting your subconscious idea of what is possible.

Begin your journey toward becoming a master student by being a master student. Get what you want naturally. Use your subconscious powers.

If you want it, be it.*

Is your goal to be the successful student who walks down the aisle, shakes the college president's hand, and receives a diploma? Can you visualize yourself in your cap and gown talking after the ceremony with friends and family? Can you feel your college degree in your hand?

You are the successful student in your picture. Guided by your plan for achievement, you create your success. You assess your situation, consider possibilities for moving closer to your goal, and implement the best plan you can put together. If you don't get quite as far as you expect, you take stock and try again. Because you are a successful student, you do find a way to achieve what you want.

When both your conscious and subconscious mind work together, you feel like something good is about to happen. You may not know all the answers yet, but you're confident that eventually you will find them.

Just the opposite is true when only your conscious mind agrees to help implement your plan. If your subconscious mind insists that you are an ineffective student and always will be, you're likely to subtly undermine your efforts to achieve. You may go through the motions of completing the tasks you've set up for the term, but things won't quite click. If you can't realistically imagine yourself as a successful student, it's important to recognize what's going on and talk with a counselor on your campus. Sabotaging your own success is possible but something you can learn to avoid if you want to.

*From Becoming a Master Student by D. Ellis, 1985, pp. 322–323. Copyright © 1985 by College Survival Inc. Reprinted by permission.

Implementing your plan gives you a chance to try out the new ways of thinking and acting that you've chosen to experiment with for the next few weeks. So pay attention to your thinking, and let the successful student that you are take control of your college experience this term.

Visualize the successful student that you are, and think about this question:

As I put my plan into action, how can both my conscious and subconscious mind work together to promote my success?

Thinking about your response to this question will help you implement your plan from the mindset of "being."

3. Check Your Progress Regularly

As you implement your plan, you will want to be aware of the results you get. This progress check will let you know when your plan is working and when it might make sense to make some adjustments.

For example, after you celebrate getting an "A" on a test, take a few minutes to think about how you earned it. What did you do to learn the material? How much review did you include in your study plan? Did you work alone or did you study with others?

Give the same kind of analysis to grades you're less pleased with. What could you have done to turn out a better research paper? Did you need more resources to thoroughly develop your topic? Were there writing errors you didn't catch, or guidelines for the project that you neglected to follow?

Evaluating the results you get as you put your plan into action gives you a chance to correct your course. You tried to anticipate the best way to go about your college experience this term, but perhaps reality threw in a few glitches that you didn't foresee or presented you with some unpredictable circumstances that might be best not to ignore for the future. If you use your plan as a flexible guide rather than as a mindlock, you'll be able to respond appropriately.

Insisting that plans work regardless of the initial feedback can be shortsighted. One student, wanting desperately to keep her job and attend college full-time, almost lost her chance to do either one:

"I was in my junior year and just starting to take courses in my major. I found the switch from general studies courses to business quite a shock. We covered a lot of material in depth, and we were expected to compete with one another for our grades. The amount of time I had set aside for studying in my plan was about half what I really needed.

At the same time, I wanted to keep working 30 hours a week at my job. I liked doing retail work at the sporting goods store near campus, and I thought it was good experience for someone going into business. The owner really didn't want me to cut back on my hours, and I liked having the extra money that the job brought in.

Things came to a head at midterm exam time. Though scores on my quizzes and papers for the first part of the term had been low, I thought I'd be able to make up for that with good grades on my tests. It sure didn't happen—in fact, my test grades plunged to new depths.

I finally realized that I had to make some changes. I needed to stop thinking that college would go well just because I had the self-discipline to carry out the plan I had made before the term began. The plan had a basic flaw—and until I corrected it, my status as a student was in jeopardy. So I cut my work hours to ten a week and built more study time into my schedule. It was a scramble to raise my grades with only half of the term left, but I did it. And even though my boss wasn't thrilled with my new schedule, she admitted that my working 30 hours a week under stress didn't do her business much good either."

Because this student evaluated her situation during the term, she was able to keep her job and earn the grades she needed. If she had waited until the end of the term, the results could have been much different.

Checking your progress regularly keeps you aware of the results you're getting. The grades you earn on quizzes, tests, and reports provide you with objective feedback to measure your progress. Are your efforts paying off? Do you need to make some adjustments? Informal comments from faculty, advisers, and friends can also help you know how you're doing. And don't ignore your own feelings and intuitions. You want to pay attention to all the signals.

Another important part of your progress check is noticing how motivated you feel while carrying out the tasks you've chosen. Since "success breeds success," you'll often find that progress in one area will give you the energy to go on to the next task in your plan. Sometimes, however, it's difficult to tell whether you're making progress, and pats on the back may be too far apart to keep your batteries charged. What can you do?

Reward yourself! Build some rewards into your own progress checks and celebrate your efforts when you carry out your plan. If getting ready for next week's exam in sociology requires long hours of study, reward yourself for doing what needs to be done. Did you complete all today's study activities on your sociology "to-do" list? Then end the day by getting together with a friend or making a phone call to that person you've been wanting to talk to. Or turn on the TV and watch a favorite program. When the system itself doesn't reward you regularly enough to make your progress enjoyable, then do it yourself.

Be aware of the signals that come to you from many different directions, and adjust your strategy accordingly. If your motivation is dipping, you may need more rewards. If you get a low grade in algebra, you may need to change the way you study for the class. No one likes to keep altering their way of doing things, but it's results that you're after. The point of making a plan is not just to keep yourself busy—you want to earn your college degree.

Protecting your plan, your approach to college, or your style of living can prevent you from achieving what you want. If you check your progress, you can act on the information you get. Then the choice of correcting your course or celebrating your efforts is yours!

Consider these questions:

How can I check my progress on a daily basis? On a weekly basis?

When might I be tempted to protect myself rather than correct my course?

Your responses to these questions will help you make evaluation a regular activity and alter your plan as necessary.

You put a lot of energy into figuring out what didn't work well for you in the past, and you've set up a plan to correct your course this term.

Now you're ready for action. Give some thought to what will help you turn your plan into reality by completing the statements below.

Implementing My Plan

Selecting a system of structure and support that I'm comfortable with will help me carry out my plan. Knowing what I do about myself, I'm

choosing a system in which I _____

_____

_____

_____

_____

_____

_____

_____

_____

_____

I know it's also important that I visualize my success as I work to achieve my goals. As I picture the successful student that I am this

term, I see myself _____

_____

_____

_____

_____

_____

_____

_____

_____

_____

Checking my progress regularly will keep me focused on my goals and will let me know how I'm doing. I can evaluate my progress on a daily

basis by _____

_____

_____

_____

I can check my progress on a weekly basis by _____

_____

_____

_____

When my progress is not what I want it to be, it's important that I quickly correct my course so that I can get the results I want. I realize I might be tempted to protect myself rather than make changes if

_____

_____

_____

_____

_____

_____

_____

However, I'll resist the temptation to blindly follow my plan even when it doesn't work and instead I will _____

_____

_____

_____

_____

_____

_____

_____

Now that you have thought through how you're going to proceed, you're ready to implement your plan. Carry out the tasks you've chosen, and stay open to feedback about your progress. You're ready to get on with your education!

10

Giving Yourself a Chance to Learn

Regardless of how smart you are, it's a challenge to earn a college degree. Not only do you need to meet your college's academic standards, but you also want to reach your own personal understanding of the content of your courses. You want to enjoy the process of learning.

Succeeding in college requires doing well academically. Just enrolling in classes that look interesting or signing up for the next course in your degree plan doesn't necessarily mean that all will go well. You must also figure out what you as a student, with your own individual strengths and weaknesses, can do to help yourself learn.

Paying close attention to who you are and what you bring to the academic setting, consider your approach to your coursework. Look over the list below and think about how you would answer the questions. Though students find that their responses vary, they all agree that giving these questions some serious thought is essential to their success.

Critical Issues of College Learning

1. How do I put together a course schedule that helps me do my best?

2. How do I know what is important to learn in each of my courses?

3. How much study time should I allow?

4. How can I make the most of my personal learning style?

5. How can I best use class time for learning?

6. How should I organize my daily studying?

With your initial responses to these questions in mind, let's look further into your options for addressing these issues.

1. How Do I Put Together a Course Schedule That Helps Me Do My Best?

All courses are not created equal! Not only do they differ in their requirements, but *you* differ in the interest and background you bring to each class. So finding out as much as you can about a course and about how the instructor teaches it can help you put together a balanced course load for the term.

For instance, if you know that you have good reading comprehension skills but that you tend to be a slow reader, you won't want to enroll in several courses that rely heavily on textbooks to teach their content. You may want to offset one heavy reading course with a math course and a writing course so that you'll be able to prepare for your classes and keep up with your assignments.

What if you need to take a college algebra course and you haven't used algebra since the ninth grade? You might want to balance this course, which may be difficult and require more study, with courses that come easily to you. Then you'll have the time and energy to put extra effort where it's needed.

If you have strong preferences about how you are evaluated, you may want to enroll in courses that test your understanding through papers rather than exams. Or you might look for instructors that encourage class discussion so that you can get more involved in the content of the course.

The more you know about the courses you're considering, the more informed your decision about what to take will be. But how can you find out about courses and their requirements on your campus?

You might start with your college catalog for a general description of course content and prerequisites, then follow up with a visit to a departmental office if you have questions. Many offices keep syllabuses on file for students to look over, and sometimes they even have samples of old exams. Faculty are an excellent resource, and usually they're willing to answer specific questions about courses during their office hours. The student grapevine works well, too—as long as you're sure to find out exactly what made a course "hard" or "easy" according to other students. Just as all courses are not alike, neither are students' reactions to a class or instructor.

Some students feel the best way to make good decisions about classes is to "overenroll" in courses for the term. Students intending to carry 15 credit hours initially enroll in 18 and use the first week of classes to decide what combination of courses will work best. Once they decide, they drop one course. Students who use this system maintain that there's nothing like the reality of attending a few classes to help you make the right choice, but this option does have its drawbacks. (For one, waiting for your refund can be frustrating if you need the money.)

Regardless of the method you use to choose your courses, you need to remember that balance is the key. Only you can decide what combination of courses is right for you. When you take the time to put together a good course plan for the term, you give yourself a chance to succeed with your learning.

2. How Do I Know What Is Important to Learn in Each of My Courses?

Attending classes the first week of the term can be like hiking to the edge of a cliff overlooking a deep canyon. Curious about what's ahead, you hurry on until you reach your destination. You anticipate what the view will be like and how it will feel to stand at the top of the mountain. Once there, you peer down over the rocky edge and look in wonder at the sight below. You bask for a few moments in the beauty of your surroundings, marveling at the ruggedness of the landscape.

All of a sudden you're aware that what you're standing on is a piece of rock jutting out into the air. Your curiosity and wonder turn to dismay. The question "What am I doing here?" races through your mind, immediately followed by "What's the safest way out?" You back off the cliff quickly, thankful that you've lived to tell about it.

Listening to your instructors introduce your classes on the first day can be much like peering over the edge of a cliff. You enrolled in the courses, anticipating what the classes would be about and what approach the various instructors might use to teach the content. You've thought about questions that you hope your courses will answer, and you look forward to preparing further for your future career.

Now, sitting in your sociology class, you leaf through the six-page syllabus that outlines your introduction to the study of, say, the criminal mind. You note the number of required readings for the course, then skim over the list of papers you'll need to write. The dates for three quizzes and two exams catch your attention. As you begin to read the section on volunteering two hours a week in the state prison, your mind shouts "Don't forget you also have four papers, six quizzes, and seven exams in your other courses. And chemistry has weekly labs too!" You look up from your sociology syllabus with glazed eyes. The bell rings, saving you from having to bolt from the room before the period is over. "How can I learn all this material?" you wonder. "Will I survive the semester?"

Fortunately, students do not need to complete all the work for the term during the first week. And while a lot of learning will eventually need to take place, you will not be responsible for all knowledge in the fields of sociology, chemistry, and whatever other areas your courses happen to represent.

In addition to learning what *you* want to learn, it's important to sort out what you're expected to learn in each of your classes so that you know what you're contending with during the next several weeks. How can you find this out?

• **Check the course syllabus.** You'll often find a list of course objectives that will outline the scope of the course. These objectives tell you in broad, general terms what you will need to know in order to master the content of the course.

• **Listen to your instructor.** When introducing the course, your instructor will interpret the course syllabus. Listen to what gets special attention, making note of where the instructor puts additional emphasis. Watch for further cues from the instructor throughout the term. When your instructor says "This is important for you to know" or "This discussion goes beyond what's required for the course," jot down this information so you'll remember it.

- **Attend classes.** Notice how your instructor uses class time. Do the lectures give you course content that is not available elsewhere? Or are they used simply to clarify the meaning of the text? Does your instructor take this opportunity to put the material into context and talk about its applications? Classes often reflect what the instructor wants you to be able to do with the course content by the end of the term. If you're in class, you'll be able to pick up on it.

- **Determine the purpose of your textbook.** Is your text the primary source of information for your course, or does it just supplement your instructor's lectures? Then again, maybe your text is used to provide general background for class discussion. If you're not sure how the text is used in the course, talk to your instructor about it. Once you find out, you'll know how to read and study your text. Adjust the thoroughness of your reading and note taking to fit the situation.

- **Watch for similarities between textbook assignments and classroom lectures and discussions.** When course content shows up in several different places, you can be sure it's important to learn. Suppose you read a chapter that describes the eight great themes in art, and then you attend several classes where the instructor shows slides to illustrate how artists over the centuries have developed these themes. Without even asking, you know what you will be tested on.

- **Use study questions.** If your instructor gives you questions to guide your textbook reading, you can assume that the material covered by the questions is important for you to know. If your textbook comes with questions that check your understanding of the material, talk with your instructor about how to use them. Are they an accurate representation of what you should learn, or are they either too detailed or too shallow?

- **Review assigned problems, lab experiments, and homework exercises.** Your instructor uses assignments to reinforce your learning in the course. Check with your instructor to find out if the level of difficulty is similar to what you'll have on exams. Is it easier? More difficult?

- **Talk to students who have taken the course before.** Based on their experience with the content and your instructor, what was important? How consistent were tests with discussion topics in class and homework exercises?

- **Look over old exams.** Does your college keep a file of old exams for students to review? Check with your learning center, residence hall libraries, or sorority and fraternity scholarship chairpersons to find out who keeps these materials. Or ask your instructors if they put old exams in a central location for students to study. If such exams are available, remember that it's the format of the test that helps you determine what's important to know. You will not find the same questions on your exams.

These are just some of the sources available for finding out what you need to know for each of your classes. Rather than be overwhelmed by the possibility of what you might need to learn this term, actively seek out what you're actually expected to know in each of your classes. Then you can decide what to do.

3. How Much Study Time Should I Allow?

Because each student is an individual, there's no single answer to this question. Most college catalogs say that you'll need two hours of studying outside of class for every one hour you spend in class. Does this average hold true for you? If not, why?

Many students find that the two-hour figure works well for the beginning of the term. If learning comes easily and their grades are top-notch, they can back off a little and reduce their study time. Or, if trouble pops up, they can figure out what else would make sense to do and add it to their study time.

Regardless of how this particular guideline works for you, it's important to realize that learning a particular assignment will usually follow a pattern. If you set aside enough time to keep to this pattern on a regular basis, you'll be on the right track. Here are some ground rules you can use.

First, you need a few minutes to **introduce yourself to the material.** This is a warm-up period in which you preview what you'll be learning. You might look over the chapter headings in your textbook or skim the charts and diagrams in the chapter. Or you might review your notes just before a lecture begins so you can remember what you were discussing two days before. By giving your mind a chance to absorb what it is you're going to ask it to do, you get ready to learn.

Second, you **look for a way to make the material meaningful.** Your mind needs to put this new material into the context of what you've learned before. Thoughts such as "This reminds me of . . ." or "What's really happening here is . . ." are signs that you're making sense of the new information. You're building on your previous knowledge and adding new understanding to it.

If you can't make the material meaningful on your own, don't plunge on just because you're full of self-discipline. Talk with another student, a tutor, or your instructor. Or look at another text on the topic to get an additional explanation. Make sure you have at least a basic understanding of what's going on before you move to the next step.

Third, you **organize the material** so that it will stick in your mind. Too many details blowing around like flurries in a snowstorm will get lost in your head. So you look for ways to sort out the information. How are the ideas related to one another? Can you outline the major topics and subtopics? Draw a diagram to show how one concept leads to another? Chart the similarities and differences among the ideas?

Next, you **rehearse what you've learned.** You practice problems in math, new vocabulary for your language class, or character analysis for your next short story seminar. You give yourself enough time to think about the material you're learning so that you can use the information as you need it. You allow time in your review for plenty of repetition so you can remember details later when you need them.

Finally, you sit back and **fit your new learning into the big picture.** What's the main idea here? What are all these details about? What's the glue that holds all these bits and pieces together? Just as you wouldn't like starting work on a jigsaw puzzle without first seeing the picture on the box, your mind can't keep track of a lot of new information if it doesn't have a framework to fit all the pieces into.

Follow these steps to make the most of the time you set aside for learning. When you have a system for learning, you'll find you can learn more in less time.

4. How Can I Use My Learning Style to Help Me Learn?

There are lots of different ways to go about learning. When you write a research paper, for instance, do you start by going to the library and checking to see what resources are available on certain topics? Or are you more apt to brainstorm writing ideas while eating lunch with your friends? Perhaps you prefer to mull over your options for a few days before you take any action at all.

The way you personally go about getting information and sorting it out is known as your *learning style*. Each of us has a preferred way of learning, though we are not all aware of our preferences. Sometimes students are so busy imitating how they think college learners should look and act that they don't use what would work best for them. But if you're aware of how you naturally prefer to learn, you can use this information to be a more efficient and effective student.

Filling out a learning styles inventory at your campus learning center is one way to find out more about your own style. Remember that no one style is better than any other, and that your goal is to learn more about how you prefer to learn. Your style of learning may not fit neatly into any one category or stay exactly the same in all situations. But if you know how you naturally prefer to learn, you can use the strengths of your style to help you make decisions about studying. Let's look at some of the ways students connect with new ideas and turn them into concepts they can understand and use.

Understanding New Material

College courses are packed with new information, and your job is to figure out how to take it all in. Which of these students is most like you when it comes to understanding new material?

_____ If I am reading a chapter in my history text on the Civil War and I'm running into detail after detail about the battles that were fought, I have to step back and take some time out to put things into perspective. What's going on? How do these pieces fit together? What do these battles look like on a timeline? Picturing in my mind exactly what's happening in the text doesn't win me any speed-reading awards, but it's a really important step to understanding the material. If I can't visualize what I'm reading, then I know I haven't caught on to what's important in the chapter.

Students who learn through *visualization* translate the ideas that they read and hear into pictures. What was frowned upon as daydreaming in grade school is actually a powerful tool that can help students understand and remember what they want to learn. The pictures may stay in the student's head as mental images or they may wind up as sketches in the margin of a text or notebook. Students who like to learn by visualizing not only make up their own images; they also look for illustrations of the concepts they are studying: videos, slides, and textbook graphics help these students learn.

Asking "What would this look like?" helps visualizers picture and find meaning in what they want to learn.

_____ When I'm learning new information, I like to read about it. Seeing information in print helps me make sense of what I need to understand and remember. When I took my first class in German, for instance, I really struggled with the instructor's approach to teaching a language. We spent all our class time listening to German conversation and learning to reply with appropriate responses. For homework, we listened to tapes in the language lab. While some of the students caught on right away, I felt frustrated. I needed to see what I was learning as well as hear it. Once I convinced my instructor to let me use a textbook in addition to attending class and listening to tapes, I started to learn and was able to catch up with my classmates. At last I could read about what we were doing in class and see the structure of the conversation I'd been trying to imitate.

Students who enjoy learning through the *written word* find that they understand information best when they see it in print. Reading the text before going to class helps them grasp the important ideas in the lecture and provides background information for the class discussion. Taking notes lets them put discussion ideas and their own observations into words. When studying for tests, these students might organize what they want to learn in a chart or outline so that they can see how one idea relates to another. They often use colored highlighters to isolate key words and phrases so that the printed word stands out and serves as a memory cue.

Asking "What could I read on this topic?" or "How could I write this up?" puts these students in touch with the resources they need to increase their learning.

_____ Whether or not to attend class has never really been a question for me because that's where I do most of my learning. I learn best when I hear ideas being discussed. I could spend hours with a textbook trying to get at the author's message, but put me with a group of people talking about an idea and everything falls into place. For me, listening just naturally leads to understanding. The lightbulb flashes on when I'm in the middle of a discussion and I know I've come to grips with what is important to know. And later, if I need to remember specific details for a test, I just take my mind back to the discussion and I can hear *exactly* what I need to recall.

Auditory learners like to learn through *listening*. They attend lectures, join discussion groups, and study with a partner. They skim their text before going to class, but usually save serious reading time for after the instructor discusses the material in the lecture. Because these students learn best when they give their full attention to the speaker, they often take limited notes in class. And notes taken during reading sessions may not be written at all. Instead, many auditory learners record the important information on tape, then prepare for tests by listening to their summaries.

Asking "Could we meet and talk about this?" or "How could I hear these ideas?" gives these students a chance to learn effectively.

Processing What You Learn

Just as your approach to taking in new information is part of your learning style, so is the way you choose to process it. Which of these students is most like you?

_____ I like to know the human angle of the topic I'm studying. In my sociology class where we're learning about the homeless, for instance, I want to go beyond the statistics that tell us how many homeless people there are in America and what percentage of the federal budget goes to address their needs. I want to talk about the homeless in my city and how we make choices about who gets aid and who doesn't. I want to talk about the values we hold as a nation when we designate federal money for one program and not another. A good instructor for this course is one who can share personal experiences and insights from working with this population.

Students who take a *subjective* approach to learning look at processing information in a personal way. Using their own emotions and experiences as reference points, these students get personally involved with the issues they study. They trust their intuition and sense when they're on the right track. They want instructors to back up their explanations of theory with a discussion of experiences from real-life situations. They want to know what roles people played in an event and how those people were affected by it. And these students want to understand how the information affects them personally.

Asking "How do I feel about this?" or "What impact does this have on people?" helps these students connect with the material they are trying to learn.

_____ I like structured courses that present information clearly. I enjoy taking a look at the causes of events and analyzing where particular decisions may lead. One of the best courses I've had was on the Vietnam war. My instructor, who knew how to look at what had happened with a critical view, presented data on the war in a logical, rational way. Most people who talk about Vietnam get so emotionally involved in the topic that it's difficult to get a good idea of what actually occurred. This instructor's analytical approach to the war helped me see how one event led to another.

Students who take an *objective* approach to learning like to analyze the information they're studying. They focus on the facts, trying to fit them into a logical framework. To solve problems, they organize the facts into different frameworks against which to test their solutions. The more facts they have, the more satisfied they are that they can reach a proper conclusion.

Asking "What are the facts I should be considering?" or "What's important for me to know to understand this?" leads these students to the information they need for learning.

Interacting with Ideas

Taking in new information and making sense of it are important components of how you learn. Just as important are your preferences for how you participate in learning. Which of these students is most like you?

_____ When I'm in the classroom, I like to listen and think about what is going on in the discussion. Hearing what the instructor and the other students have to say helps me form my opinion. I don't like situations where I have to worry about whether or not the instructor is going to call on me. It's not that I'm particularly shy or embarrassed about speaking in front of the class—I just prefer to talk when I'm ready.

Students who learn by *observing* take a reserved approach to the classroom, preferring to watch what's happening from the sidelines. They take information in, digest it, and react to the ideas they find. They like to take their time with learning, wanting a chance to think through their ideas carefully. Often these students look for classroom situations in which they can listen to the lecture and discussion but feel no pressure to participate. Once they've had a chance to sort through their thoughts, they like to present their ideas in writing or some other prepared form.

Asking "What do I see happening here?" or "What do others have to say about this?" prompts the thinking and the learning of these students.

_____ Whenever I want to learn, I need to be active. In class I take part in discussions because that's how I get involved with the material. Having a teacher call on me in class is good because it keeps me thinking and gives me a chance to check what I understand. Or if a friend will work math problems with me outside of class, then we can compare how we got the answer. Doing something with what I learn is important. Otherwise, my mind falls asleep and fools me into thinking that I know more than I really do!

Students who learn by *doing* like to make things happen. If they're part of a current-events class, they want to debate the issues. If they're learning about juvenile delinquents, they want to visit the local detention center. If they need to read 60 pages of history, they take notes on 3 x 5 cards or chart the information on a timeline or set up a study group. These students learn the most when they're right in the middle of solving a problem or discussing a point in class.

Asking "How can I get involved in this?" keeps these students on their toes and gives them the adrenaline they need for learning.

Once you know your preferences for learning, use this information! Do you understand new material by visualizing pictures, reading the printed word, or listening? Do you take a subjective or objective approach to processing what you learn? Do you participate in learning by observing ideas or doing something with them? Give yourself permission to do whatever works best for you. Use the strengths of your style to help yourself do what's important in each of your courses.

5. How Can I Use My Class Time for Learning?

You register for classes and pay your tuition for the term. Then you make the choice: Should I attend my classes? If you know how to use your class time for learning, the answer will definitely be *yes!*

Being in class gives you a chance to hear what the instructor has to say. You have a personal guide to point out how the content of the course developed and how one idea relates to another. Some instructors will even suggest how to go about learning the material. But what do you do while all this teaching is going on?

You think about ways to participate. You set yourself up to learn in class when you

- **prepare for class.** When you come to class prepared, even if you don't completely understand everything, you're ready to learn. You've read the background for today's discussion, and you've noted what's confusing. By preparing for class, you're making a statement: *I care about learning in this class.*

- **sit in the front and stay alert.** Sitting in front puts you close enough to the instructor to hear and makes it easier to keep your mind focused on the topic—because there are fewer distractions to catch your eye. The instructor is able to see your interest, or recognize your confusion if the going gets tough. By sitting in front and paying attention, you're making a second statement: *This subject is important to me.*

- **take notes.** In taking notes, just how much you write down and what format you use is up to you. Knowing your reason for taking notes will help you decide what's best. If you're taking notes because writing helps you stay alert, then simply listing items at a pace that keeps you focused on the discussion will do the job. If you're taking notes because the information is not available anywhere else, then you'll want to pay close attention to detail. You might want to record the ideas in an outline, indenting to organize the information under main headings. Or use the Cornell System, in which you reserve a column to the left of your notes to write key words that highlight the information. Then again, you may just want your notes to remind you that certain information is important, so you might decide to record the ideas in brief paragraphs. Whatever system you choose, taking notes makes yet another statement: *This instructor has something worthwhile to say.*

• **discuss ideas and raise questions.** Speaking up in class may seem risky. After all, you're just learning this material—how can you sound brilliant? Yet remember that none of the other students is an expert either, and that your instructor invites your participation. If teachers wanted to talk to a brick wall, they wouldn't stand in front of a classroom. So keep your stage fright in perspective, and make one last statement: *I'm willing to get involved to increase my learning.*

Not everyone who goes to class gets something from it. It is possible to physically show up and yet be absent mentally. Mulling over personal problems during class distracts your attention from the topic of the day. Coming to class unprepared makes lectures seem boring and meaningless. And there are quieter places to read the newspaper or write letters than the back of the classroom!

But you *can* use your class time wisely. If you're going to attend class, be there. Whether you connect through attention or discussion, the class can be your bridge to understanding the content of the course. Participate, and you will learn.

6. How Should I Organize My Daily Studying?

Often students give themselves little credit for what they do on a daily basis, even though it's this *everyday* effort that really produces learning. When asked if they're studying for next week's test, they say, "No, I'm just doing the reading" or "No, I'm just making up some vocabulary cards." But the truth is that they *are* studying; what they're doing on a regular basis will give them better results than their marathon cram session the night before the big event. If you think of yourself as a student preparing for the final exam from the first day of class, you'll see how important each day really is.

How do you organize your studying so that you're doing some learning every day? Start by making some decisions about the basics.

When during the Day Do I Learn Best?

You've probably noticed that your energy level rises and falls during the day. You may bounce out of bed full of vigor when the sun comes up, then mellow out in the early afternoon. Or perhaps you slowly ease into the day and peak around three o'clock. You might even be a night owl, perking up only after the sun goes down. Regardless of when it is that your energy soars, you want to use that time for learning.

Chances are you've been using this time for something other than studying. After all, it does feel a little unnatural to sit down and open a book just when your engine starts to race. But when you use this time for learning, you'll find that your mind is alert and your thinking is sharp. This is quality study time.

You'll need to use other times during the day to study, too, but you can choose tasks for those times that require less brain power. Go to the library to check into resources for your paper, or type up that theme for composition class, or meet with your group to review questions for your next test in psychology. You might even practice your Spanish vocabulary while you do your laundry.

Remember, use your best time of the day to do the learning that challenges your thinking and requires your thorough concentration, then fill in the gaps with activities that reinforce this learning.

Where Can I Learn?

Find a place to study regularly that helps you focus your attention. You need to be comfortable, but not overly relaxed. You want this place to signal your brain and body that learning is about to take place.

Your choice of a study area is a personal decision. Give some thought to what works well for you as well as what distracts you. How much noise can you tolerate? Will people moving around the room interfere with your concentration? How does studying near a telephone affect you?

You don't want to check into a monastery, but you do want to put yourself in a place where you can learn effectively in a limited amount of time. You can't study 24 hours a day, so the studying you do needs to pay off.

Look at the one or two places you currently study. Do they support your learning? Does just being there, where you've spent so much time studying, automatically remind you to focus on learning? Are these places away from the TV, people, and general commotion? Do they have good lighting and ventilation? Give yourself a chance to learn by finding a study area that meets your needs. Let your choice remind you, your friends, and your family that studying is a high priority and that it demands your complete attention.

How Should I Use My Time?

You want your study time to pay off. So it's important that you give careful consideration to what activities will support your learning and how to go about them.

Plan what you're going to learn. First, find out what's important to learn in each of your courses (we discussed several sources for this information previously in this chapter). Next, break down these academic goals into specific tasks (we discussed how to do this in Chapter 8). Monitor your progress as you carry out these tasks so that you'll know whether you're using your time well. Your plan will help you pace your activities, too—constantly reminding you of what is important, and giving you a structure that helps you get things done on time.

When you're organizing your daily studying, you'll need to distribute your learning time over a period of hours and days. Gear the length of individual study sessions to fit your attention span, and then give your brain several chances to connect with the material. Forget about studying biology for eight hours on Saturday—you'll take too little away from this marathon session to make your effort worthwhile. Study in shorter sessions instead, respecting your brain's need to focus and review. Work to understand the concepts you're studying, then rehearse what you want to remember. Give yourself plenty of time for review so that you can show what you've learned in a test situation.

When you need to use long sessions, try to give your brain some variety. Change subjects when possible, moving from reading economics to solving trig problems to drafting an essay. If you must stay with the same course, at least vary your activity. Do some reading and outlining, then practice what you're learning. Give yourself a lecture on cell division, or draw an illustration of mitosis. And work regular short breaks into your schedule—you're asking a lot of your brain, so treat it with care!

To give yourself a chance to learn, figure out how you want to respond to each of the questions in the list of Critical Issues of College Learning. Each asks you to make a decision about how you'll handle the process of learning in your courses. Coming up with answers puts you in charge of your education.

Looking in the Mirror

Take a look at each of the Critical Issues of College Learning. How are you choosing to answer these questions?

1. How do I put together a course schedule that helps me do my best?

   For me, a balanced course plan involves _____

   _____

   _____

   _____

   _____

   _____

   _____

   _____

   _____

Use your current course plan as an example. Is it a balanced plan?

Why or why not? _____

_____

_____

_____

_____

_____

2. How do I know what is important to learn in each of my courses?

When I'm not sure what is important to learn in my classes, I

_____

_____

_____

_____

_____

_____

_____

_____

_____

3. How much study time should I allow?

    For the classes I'm taking this term, I study approximately

    _____ hours a week. I use this time to _____

    _____

    _____

    _____

    _____

    _____

    _____

    _____

    _____

    I know I've set aside enough time to learn when _____

    _____

    _____

    _____

    _____

    I know I need to use my time for learning differently when _____

    _____

_____

_____

_____

_____

_____

Do you currently have enough time to learn for your classes?

_____

4. How can I make the most use of my personal learning style?

   From what I know about my preferences for learning, it would help

   me to set up learning situations in which I can _____

   _____

   _____

   _____

   _____

   _____

   _____

   _____

   _____

5. How can I best use my class time for learning?

   How do you make your classes a good learning time for you? What else could you do that would help you gain more from class?

   I learn in class when _____

   _____

   _____

   _____

   _____

   _____

   I'd like to increase the amount I learn in class by _____

   _____

   _____

   _____

   _____

6. How should I organize my daily studying?

   How, when, and where I study makes a difference in how much I

   learn. I organize my daily studying by _____

   _____

   _____

_____

_____

_____

_____

_____

_____

_____

In summary, I give myself the best chance to learn when I _____

_____

_____

_____

_____

_____

_____

_____

_____

_____

11

Negotiating Your Path to Success

Success on demand. How available is it?

Changing your approach to college takes time, energy, and self-discipline. If you've made a plan and you're doing your part to carry it out, shouldn't success naturally follow? Don't you deserve to get what you're after?

Success is definitely possible, but sometimes the path to it is not as straight as you expect. You may find that you have to negotiate some curves along your path to success. Consider what writer Andrew Matthews has to say.[10]

> When setting out for a goal, it is worthwhile remembering the way things work on this planet. Nothing travels in straight lines. No goals are achieved without setbacks.
>
> When the tide comes in, it comes in a bit and goes out a bit, but gradually it makes its way in. When a tree grows, it loses leaves from time to time, and each time it grows a few extra to compensate for the losses. The net result is that the tree gets bigger but it does not do [so] without some loss and some struggle. The way things work on this planet is that setbacks are a part of the plan of things.
>
> Successful people are not that brilliant or talented or unique. They simply have a grasp of the way things work and realize that their own progress will be in accordance with the principles that govern everything else around them.

They realize that we reach our goals by continually correcting. We get off-course, correct, and get back on course. Ships do it. Rockets and missiles do it. Correct. Correct. Correct.*

Correcting requires recognizing that everything is not going smoothly yet. As much as you want to succeed, something is still out of whack. You can see signs of improvement, but you're not quite there. How can you get what you want?

Do some troubleshooting. Start negotiating your path to success by putting your cards on the table. Ask yourself:

☑ What's holding me back?

☑ Who's on my team?

☑ How can I communicate what I want?

Let's take a closer look at each of these questions.

What's Holding Me Back?

If you can figure out what the problem is, you may be able to do something about it. Take Mike's situation, for instance:

"I was living at home and commuting to the university each day. I was on probation, but I knew I could toe the line if I set my mind to it. And since my plan had been working for about five weeks, I was feeling pretty confident that this term was going to come out right.

Then things fell apart at home again. My parents were fighting every night. They started as soon as my Dad walked in the door from work and they didn't stop until he left the next morning. With all that yelling and door slamming going on, I couldn't think straight. No matter how hard I tried to study, I just couldn't concentrate. I thought a lot about moving out, but I didn't have enough money for an apartment. Financial aid was out of the question, and I couldn't keep my grades up if I worked more hours on my job. My situation was going downhill fast."

*From Being Happy by A. Matthews, 1988, p. 84. Copyright © 1988 by Price Stern Sloan. Reprinted by permission.

Living at home was holding Mike back. With parents on their way to divorce, the tension in his house was too great for Mike to study. As difficult as the situation was, however, Mike found that it was possible to deal with the problem. Leaving the house and studying at the library until late at night gave him a chance to salvage his grades for the current term. Talking with a counselor helped him sort out the emotional mess he was part of. Then he focused on what to do for the long run. After considering several options, Mike rented a bedroom at a friend's house and finished his degree.

If you know what's holding you back, you can put your energy into dealing with it. Does your personal life make you feel like the victim in a soap opera? Do your finances chain you to the workplace? Does your academic background keep you from passing "GO"? Are you surrounded by people who would just as soon you didn't get a college degree? Does studying take more time than you have?

There are ways to address any of these situations. Personal counselors are great at helping students figure out how to manage current problems and prevent turmoil in the future. Sometimes your financial aid office can connect you with resources you didn't know were available or can at least make you aware of what your options are. Community colleges and resource centers can put you in touch with the background you need to make it in college courses. And chances are your campus learning assistance center has courses, workshops, and one-on-one help for becoming a more efficient learner.

Help is available to deal with almost anything that's holding you back. It is true that sometimes the options for dealing with your situation will seem less than fantastic. In fact, you may not be excited about any of them. Maybe getting your degree is going to take more time than you hoped. Or maybe your lifestyle as a student will have to be different than you expected. But talking over your situation with other people will keep you aware of all your alternatives. The choice of what you do is then yours.

Who's on My Team?

What kind of support do you have for what you're trying to do? How helpful are you to yourself? Who are your partners and allies?

Since you're the one you have the most contact with, let's look at you first.

Team Member Group 1: Me, Myself, and I

Are you your best friend, or do you tend to be your worst enemy? How supportive are you of your efforts to get off probation and on with your education?

What you say to yourself as you think about your situation makes a big difference in the kind of support you're giving yourself. If the monologue going on in your head runs like "You stupid idiot! How'd you get in this mess in the first place?" you're not much help to yourself. Follow it up with a few comments like "Nothing I do makes much difference" and "I'm just a loser putting in time on campus" and you're well on your way to defeat.

You can become a supportive member of your team by monitoring your self-talk. Coach yourself. Get words running through your mind that will help you cope with the hard parts of life. Look at the difference between styles of self-talk in the following situations:

Situation: Test in German on Friday

Negative Self-Talk:	"You make yourself look like you don't belong in college when you screw up on these vocabulary tests. Stop being such a jerk and get a perfect score this time. You know you should be able to do it."
Coaching Self-Talk:	"I can do well on this test. I need to make vocabulary cards and review them three times a day. Then I'll be ready to walk in, take the test, and do the best I can."

Situation: Problems with Large Assignments

Negative Self-Talk:	"You know how you are with these projects. You'll leave it to the last minute and then you won't think anything you do is good enough to turn in. You always fall through with the big stuff and your grades show it."
Coaching Self-Talk:	"I know it's important for me to break down this project. There are several different parts to it. By working on one piece of it each day this week, I'll get it done on time. I'll start by going to the library at three o'clock today."

Negative self-talk puts you down and focuses on the problem. When you switch to coaching self-talk, you shift your attention to staying calm and coping with the problem. You keep the situation in perspective and tell yourself what you need to do.

If supportive self-talk doesn't come naturally, practice it. Watch for situations in which you tend to put yourself down. When you anticipate difficulty in reaching a goal or see that you're in a situation that has given you trouble in the past, use that as a signal to coach yourself. Don't contribute to your own defeat just because you know that losing is possible—help yourself be a winner!

Team Member Group 2: Friends

You can go it alone, but it won't be much fun. So let's get some other people involved in supporting your success. Who do you want on your team?

Look for people who are "energy chargers." These people have lots of get up and go, and they pull you along with them. Life is full, the student experience is great, and something exciting is bound to happen today!

You know people like this. You meet them on the first day of classes and they're talking about the great courses they've got—with fantastic teachers to match! Dr. A's a famous scientist who performs unpredictable experiments in class. Dr. B's a smooth talker capable of convincing entire mega-sections to volunteer as subjects for his psychology research. Dr. C's a comedian who has political science students chuckling through the entire class.

Perhaps you also know some "energy zappers." No matter how early or late in the term it is, these people are tired. Life is awful. Their cars break down driving into campus—so they always have to park in the $50-per-minute lot. Their class schedules are outrageous, their teachers are far past their prime, and their assignments will take years to complete. Soon the details of their dismal days get lost in the whir of their whining, and you realize you're exhausted too.

Who you think you are and how you think, feel, and act are influenced by other people. This influence is so subtle that often you don't even notice it. Yet if all the other students in the back of the classroom are slumped down in their chairs, you probably won't remain sitting on the edge of yours for long. And if no one you live with ever opens a book, you may soon feel it's crazy to study. The opposite is also true. If everyone you know is thinking about how to get the most out of their time in college, you too will pick up on that theme. Even success is contagious!

The people on your team are important to you because they help you keep on track. When your motivation starts to waiver, they remind you why it is you're doing all this. When you're stuck about what to try next, they give you ideas to consider. Many teams work informally—the team members just naturally support each other because they're together a lot. Other teams are more structured. Students set aside time to meet once a week with the other people in their team. They report on how they're doing and brainstorm possibilities for getting over the rough spots. Regardless of the style, teams make a difference.

Surround yourself with energy. Look for students whose lives are working for them. It's not that they don't have problems—everybody does. But these people take life in stride and keep moving closer to what they want for themselves. Find them, and get them on your team.

Team Member Group 3: Staff Allies in Campus Resource Offices

There are staff all across campus who exist to support your success. Though their titles may vary, these people all want to help you earn your college degree.

Which of these people might be helpful to have on your team?

____ academic advisers: provide information about courses, registration, eligibility for majors, and requirements for graduation. *They understand how things work on your campus.*

____ career consultants: match your interests with college majors and possible careers; keep track of career opportunities and job market trends. *They can help you connect with your future.*

____ financial aid officers: gather information on all types of financial aid and support for students in higher education. *They know what type of assistance you qualify for and can help you apply for it.*

___ learning consultants: assist you in finding out how you learn best and how to be an efficient and effective student. *They can help you achieve your academic goals.*

___ librarians: inform you about services available at the library and about the resources that will best meet your needs. *They can help you get the most out of your time in the library.*

___ ombudspersons: know how to troubleshoot just about any bureaucratic snarl you can get tangled up in. *They can get action when you need it.*

___ personal counselors: offer help in dealing with personal situations or choices that are troubling you. *They can help you put the fun back into college.*

___ resource lab staff: assist you with computers and other instructional media to reinforce your learning. *They can connect you with academic support materials.*

___ student employment coordinators: know what job opportunities are available both on and off campus. *They can save you time in hunting down a part-time job.*

Your campus may have additional personnel who can help you out. Ironically, on many campuses the real issue is not whether there are resources available to support the students—but whether students will use the resources.

Many students, first-year students in particular, struggle with whether they should ask anyone for assistance. They may feel shy about going to offices that they're unfamiliar with, or uncertain about what to ask once they're in the door. Some hope that they're already doing the right thing, or that the problem will just take care of itself. And some feel that since they're adults they should be able to handle everything on their own. After all, what are they suggesting when they ask for help? That they might not be up to the college experience? That they really don't know all the answers? In their need to be self-reliant, these students are forgetting the value of being part of a team.

Just as presidents have advisers and athletes have coaches, students in higher education have consultants who can offer them guidance and support.

So when you're negotiating your path to success, consider including some staff members from various campus resource units. Balance your independence with a willingness to use any resource that will help you get what you want. Put your energy into getting the best support team possible.

How Can I Communicate What I Want?

You know what you want and you've got your support team in place. What else is involved in negotiating your path to success?

You need to be able to stand up for yourself and communicate your wants, needs, and feelings in a way that's respectful to both yourself and others. You want to be able to interact with people on campus in a positive way.

The skills of positive communication are best known as "assertive behavior." Your goal is to meet your needs without denying the rights of others. You want to be clear, direct, and respectful.

Compare assertive behavior with some other forms of campus communication. Who has the greatest chance of getting what he or she wants?

Passive student: "I wish Dr. Smith would explain her grading policy. It's so hard to please her—she never likes what I do."

Aggressive student: "This was an impossible assignment! I've put hours of work into this research paper and it's not fair of you to give me a low grade."

Assertive student: "I'm working for a top grade on this paper. When it's convenient for you, could we look over the draft together? I'd like to know if I'm on the right track with the assignment."

Obviously what you say has an impact on the type of response you get. By talking to someone other than Dr. Smith about her grading policy, the passive student may never understand how this particular instructor evaluates student work. And crying "Poor me!" won't help her know how to go about her next assignment. The aggressive student will probably fare no better. Although this student does talk directly to the instructor, announcing that the instructor gives impossible assignments and grades unfairly is a poor way to begin a discussion. Only the assertive student increases the possibility of something good happening. This request specifically states what the student wants and shows respect for the instructor.

Here are four guidelines for speaking from *Developing Positive Assertiveness,* written by Sam Lloyd.[11] Notice how you can open communication doors when you choose your words carefully.

Use "I" Statements Rather Than "You" Statements

Rather than telling an adviser "You always make registration so difficult!" try "I find all these details confusing." And instead of telling an instructor "You set impossible standards in this course!" try "I'm not sure how to meet this criterion for my project."

Use Factual Descriptions Instead of Judgments or Exaggerations

If you tell your adviser "I'll never graduate if you keep putting all these degree requirements in front of me!" you are far less likely to get a helpful response than if you ask "Exactly how many hours of math will I need for this particular degree program?" And insisting to an instructor that "Giving me a 'C' on this paper without writing any comments is another example of your sloppy grading!" closes the door on the possibility of obtaining information that will move you closer to your goal of graduation, while saying "The grade on my essay tells me I'm doing average work but doesn't give me any clues about how to improve. What do you suggest?" leaves the door wide open.

Notice how factual descriptions help keep the tone of your meeting conversational? You're inviting the other person to respond to your request, not your judgment.

Show Ownership of Thoughts, Feelings, and Opinions

Notice the difference between saying to an adviser "A fair policy would let me transfer these credits!" and saying "I'd like my work at my other college to be taken into consideration." See how owning your thoughts, feelings, and opinions keeps the focus on you and what you want? Also, ownership gives you a chance to express yourself honestly. Rather than complaining "She makes me angry!" admit "I get angry when I can't figure out the assignment." And since ownership helps you avoid making accusations, it reduces the likelihood of a rebuttal that could pull the conversation in another direction.

Make Clear, Direct Requests When You Want Others to Do Something

Rather than hinting to your roommate that "It sure would be nice if it were quiet enough to study here!" say "I need some quiet so that I can study. Could you help me out by turning off your stereo for one hour?" Or rather than saying "I sure wish I knew what you wanted us to write about!", ask "Can I stop in during your office hour tomorrow and talk about a short list of topics I'm considering for this paper?"

Notice how specific requests make it clear what it is you're asking for? This increases the chance that you'll get a response, and it ups the odds that the response will be the one you want.

Choosing your words carefully helps you get what you want. And because you're treating people with respect, they're more likely to want to help you out. If you'd like more practice with assertive behavior, check for workshops and seminars on your campus or read one of the many books on this topic. Developing good communication skills is worth whatever time and effort it takes. After all, it's your path to success that you're negotiating.

As you carry out your plan and work toward your success, what holds you back? What obstacles are in your path?

Sometimes my success seems just beyond my reach. What holds me

back is _____

_____

_____

_____

_____

_____

_____

_____

_____

_____

I've thought of some ways to deal with what holds me back. I would

like to _____

_____

_____

_____

_____

_____

_____

_____

Take a look at what kind of support you have for getting off probation and on with your education. How helpful are the members of your team? Consider the support you give yourself as well as the support you get from friends and staff in campus resource offices.

Team Member Group 1: Me, Myself, and I

What kind of team member are you? How do you help yourself? How do you sabotage your efforts? What does your self-talk sound like?

When I think about myself as a member of my support team, I think I

help myself when I _____

_____

_____

_____

_____

_____

_____

_____

I'm my own worst enemy when I _____

_____

_____

_____

_____

_____

_____

_____

_____

My self-talk consists of statements that _____

_____

_____

_____

_____

_____

_____

_____

Team Member Group 2: Friends

What influence do your friends have on your success? Are you surrounded by energy chargers? energy zappers? Do you have a formal or informal support network with your friends?

As I think about friends and the kind of support they give me, I realize

that _____

_____

_____

_____

_____

_____

_____

_____

_____

Team Member Group 3: Allies in Campus Resource Offices

As you consider the staff available on campus to support your success, which are currently on your team? Which would you like to add? What can these staff members offer you?

The staff in my campus resource offices _____

_____

_____

_____

_____

_____

_____

Interacting with people on campus is a vital part of negotiating your path to success. Give a brief description of a typical situation on your campus that would require you to use your communication skills. What choices would you face as a communicator? How could you respond to this situation passively? Aggressively? Assertively? Write your responses below.

Situation:

_____

_____

_____

Passive response:

_____

_____

_____

Aggressive response:

_____

_____

_____

Assertive response:

_____

_____

_____

Think about your experience with negotiating your success on campus. How would you describe your communication skills? Do you usually come across as passive, aggressive, or assertive?

As a communicator on campus, I think my current style is best de-

scribed as _____

_____

_____

_____

_____

_____

_____

One way to improve my style would be _____

_____

_____

_____

_____

_____

_____

_____

12

Managing Your Choices

You began this book with the hope of finding an approach to college that would work for you. How's it going? Where are you in the process of getting off probation and on with your education?

If you've read the chapters and thought about how to use the ideas, then you've taken steps to deal with your probationary status. If you've devised a plan for this college term and are currently putting it into action, then you're definitely taking charge of your future. You have your team to support your efforts and your assertion skills to help campus negotiations go smoothly. What else can contribute to your success?

You can choose to make choices.

Making choices is critical because change usually meets with resistance in one form or another. Remember how you were bombarded by interruptions during the first week of your new study schedule? If you sat down to study right after supper, that's when the telephone rang. "But I always call you in the evening!" was your friend's response to your new routine. If you decided to attend all your early morning classes, that's when your alarm clock broke or your car wouldn't start or your roommate permanently moved into the bathroom. If you adjusted your work hours so that you could get your assignments done before going to class, that's when your boss said "This is an emergency. You've got to come in even if these hours aren't on your schedule."

Just wanting something to be different in your life doesn't make it so. You can expect resistance in all shapes and sizes. Even people who initially cheer your efforts will sometimes balk when they see what a change actually entails. Parents who've been pleading with you to "do something about your grades" may suddenly pull back their support when they realize you can't visit home quite as often. Friends excited about your recent successes may look noticeably less enthused if you hesitate to join them for their next spur-of-the-moment party.

It's easiest to respond to this resistance without thinking. Relying on habit to tell you what to do, you might just shelve your books and go home for the weekend after all or join one more weeknight party. Responses like "Well, I guess I can talk to you for just a few minutes" get telephone conversations underway. Or thinking "Maybe it won't matter if I miss class this one time" might send you back to bed to catch a few more winks. But you have acted out these patterns over and over before, so you know from experience that the few minutes on the phone somehow turn into hours and that the one missed class somehow adds up to six or seven. That's what happens when habits make choices for you.

Making the big decision to get off probation is one thing; making the small choices to give your plan a chance to work is quite another. According to Shad Helmstetter, author of *Choices*,[12] it is only when people exercise their right to choose that they can also begin to exercise their right to change. Getting started is not as simple as it sounds, however, because choosing may not come naturally.

> The principle reason why we fail to make many of the choices we should be making is that we fail to recognize them as choices in the first place. Because of the programming we receive, it is entirely possible to grow up almost unaware that if we're not making choices for ourselves, we are then living out the results of the programming we receive from others. We are not thinking for ourselves. Others are doing it for us.*

The first step in choosing to make choices, then, is to be aware of what your choices are. Talk back to the chatter in your head that

From Choices by S. Helmstetter, 1989, p. 69. Copyright © 1989 by Pocket Books. Reprinted by permission.

says "But this is how you are and this is how you do things." Tell yourself that you have a choice about what you do. Ask yourself these questions:

1. What's the choice?

2. What are the consequences?

3. How do I want to manage this choice?

Making a conscious choice puts you in charge. The more you're aware of what your choices are, the more likely you are to make the right one. Let's take a look at how you can use this process.

Situation:

The telephone rings while you're working on your math problems.

Choices:

1. Answer the telephone.

2. Don't answer the telephone.

3. Answer and set up a time to talk later.

4. Go study in the library so you won't be around the telephone.

Consequences:

Answering the telephone:	I'll find out who's on the phone and what they want.
	My concentration will be interrupted.
	I might not finish my homework before class.
	I won't know if I need to ask my instructor questions about the homework.
	I might not be ready for Friday's quiz.
Not answering:	I'll finish my math.
	I might miss an important call.
	I'll be curious about who called.

Answer and set time to talk later:	Person might think I'm rude if I don't talk right now.
	Person might not be available to talk later.
Go to the library:	I'll be interrupted by people walking around.
	Walking to the library will use up some of my study time.

Managing My Choice

I like to know who's calling me and what they want, but I can't afford to be interrupted during my study time. And I'm afraid I might not have enough willpower to hang up if I answer and try to set a time to talk later. The library is too noisy to be a good study place for me, so I'm better off working at home. For now, I am going to stop answering the telephone during my study sessions. I will take the phone off the hook so that I won't be bothered by its ringing. I'll start saving for an answering machine so that I can handle this choice differently in the future. With my answering machine I will always know who's trying to reach me and I won't miss out on calls or my study time.

When you go through the process of managing your choices, you consciously choose what you are going to do. Rather than react in ways that no longer help you get what you want for yourself, you choose what makes sense for you in a particular situation. You consider your alternatives and you think about why one option is better than another. Habits no longer run your life.

Once you've made the choice to choose, take another important step. Give your choices support. Helmstetter describes how you can do this.

When you support your *primary* choice with other choices, you create a *team* of choices. Each of them works together to support, defend and build up the others like the players on a football team. Each player has his own position to play, but all of them work together to reach the final specific objective of getting the ball across the goal line. . . .

An example of this is the student who makes the choice to do better in school. But that one choice, no matter how important it may be, will seldom succeed standing on its own. It needs a team of supportive choices on its side.

Primary choice: **I choose to do better in school.**
Support team choices:
- The choice to improve study skills and habits.
- The choice to spend more time studying.
  The choice to cut down on activities that get in the way of school-work.
- The choice to use better concentration, listening skills, and focus in class.
- The choice to reward yourself when you do well.
- The choice to continue regardless of difficulties along the way.*

Many times good choices don't have a chance to win because we don't give them the support they need. Are some of your primary choices floundering because they're standing all alone? Maybe you've set aside time to study each night but you haven't thought about how to make your effort pay off. Or maybe you've vowed to stop procrastinating but haven't made any plan to break your cycle of waiting until the last minute to get things done. As you think about what makes college learning difficult for you, are you backing up your primary choice to earn a college degree with choices that help you deal with these difficulties?

Remember that "it is the big choices we make that set our direction. It is the smallest choices we make that get us to the destination."** Give your choices the support they need so that you can achieve your goals.

Resolving to recognize and support your choices may be the most important decision you ever make. When you manage your choices, you continue the journey from where you are to where you want to be. You set into motion your decision to get off probation and on with your education.

---

*From Choices by S. Helmstetter, 1989, pp. 197–199. Copyright © 1989 by Pocket Books. Reprinted by permission.

**From Choices by S. Helmstetter, 1989, p. 201. Copyright © 1989 by Pocket Books. Reprinted by permission.

Earlier in the book you looked at what makes learning in college difficult. In light of what you now know about managing choices, consider how you might handle one of these situations. Here's an example:

Situation:

Learning in college is difficult when you're unhappy with the institution you're attending.

What's the Choice?

Either I can stay at this college,
or I can leave this college.

What Are the Consequences?

Staying at this college means working on making it a better place for me to get my degree. I need to support my choice by

- finding an adviser who knows the system and can help me with my degree plan.

- checking on class sizes before I enroll in a specific section so that I'll have a chance to get the individual attention I need.

- making use of the student grapevine to find out who the good instructors are.

- joining an organization so that I can get to know some students who have interests similar to mine.

If I leave, I need to consider my alternatives for getting a degree and figure out how to make a change. I can support my choice by:

- investigating which colleges in this state would be a good fit for me.

- finding out the application and transfer procedures for the college I would like to attend.

- talking with a counselor about how to break the news to my parents that I don't want to continue at this college.

- making sure that I follow the correct exit procedures so that I leave this college in good standing.

How Do I Want to Manage This Choice?

I want to transfer to another college. With two years to go before I earn my degree, I'd like to be in a place that's a better match for my background and my interests. I'm tired of swimming upstream trying to make this place work. I would rather use my energy to learn. Although this change will not be easy for my parents to accept, I think it's important that I choose my future; I'll talk with a counselor about how to discuss my choice with them.

Which of the following factors make learning in college difficult for you? Use the choice management process to do some problem solving. Check off one situation you want to work with. Then continue to fill in the items below.

Situation

_____ Learning in college is difficult when personal factors interfere with my performance.

_____ Learning in college is difficult when I have problems with my courses.

_____ Learning in college is difficult when my approach to studying does not bring good results.

_____ Learning in college is difficult when I'm not really sure I want to be in college.

What's the Choice?

Either

_____

_____

_____

Or

_____

_____

_____

What Are the Consequences of Each?

If I choose to _____ ,

then what will happen is _____

_____

_____

_____

_____

_____

_____

If I choose to _____ ,

then what will happen is _____

_____

_____

_____

_____

_____

How Do I Want to Manage This Choice?

_____

_____

_____

_____

_____

_____

Choosing and supporting your choices is your key to getting what you want for yourself.

Afterword

Is there life after probation?

Up to this point you've been putting so much energy into changing your academic status that you probably haven't given much thought to what comes next. But life does go on, so let's look at some of the possibilities that may occur. What might your future hold?

1. You Are Suspended

This is not the future that you had in mind when you sat down to read this book. Yet things didn't work out. What can you do?

Start by remembering that suspension is an event and that, just like with probation, you can choose your reaction to it. Will you let the news devastate you and make you feel like you're unfit company for even your cat? Will you promptly forget all your past accomplishments and successes?

I hope not. As disappointing as the news is, you want to keep this event in perspective. Can you figure out what happened? In what specific ways did you not meet your college's standards for continuing your education? Do you know what keeps you from being successful in your program? What can you do about it?

Once you know what went wrong, you have several choices to consider. Do you want to continue working on a degree? Where would be the best place for you to do that? If you feel strongly about continuing at the college you've been attending, what are their conditions for readmission? Is part-time study in an evening or weekend program available? Or, if you're not sure that taking college courses makes sense at this point, what else would you like to do? Is this your chance to try something different for a while?

Maybe you want to postpone your decision about higher education for the moment and do some thinking. Faculty regularly take time out for thinking—they call it "taking a sabbatical." A semester or a year away from the college gives them an opportunity to travel, write a book, start new research, or work with colleagues at another university. In short, sabbaticals give faculty some breathing time. The result is renewed energy and a fresh contribution to their area of study. Students can take sabbaticals too. You can leave campus and then continue your education at another time or place. If you're committed to learning, there's a way.

Give yourself a chance to sort out what your choices are. Talking to a counselor, adviser, or good friend will help you expand your options. Planning what you're moving toward will make it easier to deal with your suspension. So put your energy into figuring out what's next. Then go for it.

2. You Continue on Probation

You did well enough to buy yourself another chance. What changes did you make that improved your results this term? What additional changes might be in order? Is there anything specific that still holds you back?

Celebrate your progress, then take a careful look at what makes sense for the new term. Take stock of your situation. Look back at what we've been talking about. What didn't you do? What did you do that you could do even better? What else do you want to try? Choose your next steps, and continue to back up your choices with specific plans.

3. You're off Probation

This is what you've been working for! You can look ahead to a new term knowing that you've found a way to get the results you want. How did you do it? What works for you? And what do you do now?

Celebrate, then celebrate some more! No one gets off probation without real effort. Congratulations!

Then shift your focus to the new term. How will you repeat your success? What made a difference for you? Plan your progress just as conscientiously as you did before, taking nothing for granted. This time things will go a little easier because experience is on your side. You've learned to notice the "yellow alerts" and the "red alerts" that tell you when to correct your course. And best of all, you've learned to act on them!

The process you used to get off probation and on with your education is one that you'll find useful for the rest of your life. You won't always be a student, but you will always have a chance to be a learner. Balancing that seesaw between failure and success is an act you'll get to do over and over again. Now you know how to do it!

References

1. Quoted in C. Hyatt and L. Gottlieb, *When Smart People Fail* (New York: Penguin Books, 1987), p. 232.

2. M. E. Larson, "Humbling Cases for Career Counselors," *Phi Delta Kappan 54* (1983): 374.

3. Hyatt and Gottlieb, *When Smart People Fail*.

4. S. Emery, *Actualizations* (Garden City, New York: Dolphin Books, 1978), pp. 195–196.

5. Hyatt and Gottlieb, *When Smart People Fail*.

6. W. Bridges, *Transitions* (New York: Addison-Wesley, 1980), p. 9.

7. Ibid.

8. A. Scheele, *Skills for Success* (New York: Ballantine Books, 1979), pp. 3–6.

9. D. Ellis, *Becoming a Master Student* (Rapid City, S. Dak.: College Survival, Inc. 1985).

10. A. Matthews, *Being Happy* (Los Angeles: Price Stern Sloan, 1988).

11. S. Lloyd, *Developing Positive Assertiveness* (Los Altos, Calif.: Crisp Publications, 1988), p. 32.

12. S. Helmstetter, *Choices* (New York: Pocket Books, 1989).

To the owner of this book:

I hope that you have been significantly influenced by *Turning Point*. I'd like to know as much about your experiences with the book as you care to offer. Your comments can help me make it a better book for future readers.

School: _____ Instructor's name:_____

Address of school (city, state, and zip code): _____

1. What I like most about this book is: _____

_____

_____

_____

2. What I like least about this book is: _____

_____

_____

_____

3. How much personal value did you find in the "Looking in the Mirror" sections?

_____

_____

4. Specific suggestions for improving the book: _____

_____

_____

5. The name of the course in which I used this book: _____

_____

6. In the space below—or in a separate letter, if you'd care to write one—please let me know what other comments about the book you'd like to make. I welcome your suggestions!

Optional:

Your name: _____ Date: _____

May Wadsworth quote you, either in promotion for *Turning Point,* or in future publishing ventures?

Yes: _____ No: _____

Sincerely,

Joyce D. Weinsheimer

FOLD HERE

NO POSTAGE
NECESSARY
IF MAILED
IN THE
UNITED STATES

BUSINESS REPLY MAIL
FIRST CLASS   PERMIT NO. 34   BELMONT, CA

POSTAGE WILL BE PAID BY ADDRESSEE

Joyce D. Weinsheimer
Wadsworth Publishing Company
10 Davis Drive
Belmont, CA 94002

FOLD HERE